Obama Will Win,
but Romney Will Be President

How Political Parties Target Electoral College
Votes to Win Presidential Elections

৵৽৵৽৵

A Historical Analysis of Every U.S. Presidential Election
and the Events That Influenced Them

Everett E. Murdock PhD

H.O.T. Press

H.O.T. Press
Ojai, California 93023
www.hotpresspublishing.com
Established 1984

ISBN: 0-923178-12-0
ISBN-13: 978-0-923178-12-3

For Zoe,
Without whom this book would not exist,
and without whom I would not exist.

Acknowledgments

I had planned to acknowledge all of the books on U.S. history that provided me with background information while I was writing this book, but I soon realized that would be an impossible task because I've been reading books on U.S. history all my life. Let me just say I am truly indebted to anybody who has written anything about U.S. history. I assume they did it simply because they are, like me, interested in the history of our country.

I am also indebted to those who took the time to put information about U.S. history on the internet. Once again, I started to list them, but found the list growing into the hundreds (and even then I knew I was leaving a bunch of them out). So I will just say this: if you've ever put anything about U.S. history on the internet, I probably read it while researching this book, and I am therefore, indebted to you.

Contents

Introduction
He Who Wins May Lose

It's a tried-and-true old saying: if you want to know what the future will bring, study the past. Studying the past, we learn that **in four U.S. presidential elections, the candidate who won the most votes did not get to be president**. It looks like it might well happen again in 2012.

The polls are all saying the U.S. 2012 presidential election will be close. In the last close presidential election, **Al Gore won the popular vote by 543,895 votes**, but George Bush got to be president. Why? Because despite Gore's win of the popular vote, Bush got five more votes than Gore in the Electoral College, accumulating 271 electoral votes, only one vote more than the 270 required to be elected president.

After studying the history of all of the U.S. presidential elections, and analyzing current voting patterns in the United States, I believe the same thing is going to happen again in 2012. **Barack Obama will win the popular vote, but Mitt Romney will become the forty-fifth president of the United States of America**.

In fact, after analyzing the history of the nation's voting patterns, state by state, region by region, and after looking at the latest 2012 public polls, it seems quite possible that Barack Obama will win the popular vote by as much as **one million votes** and yet not get enough votes in the Electoral College to be president.

In this book, I analyze each of the nation's presidential elections, and in each case, I will discuss the role the Electoral College system played in determining who got to be president.

My analysis of those past presidential elections and a study of the role the Electoral College played, leads me to conclude that once again, in 2012, the candidate who wins the popular vote will not get to be president.

Chapter One

The Origins of the Electoral College System

How is it possible that a candidate can win the popular vote and yet not be elected president? The answer lies within the archaic and complex structure of something known as **the Electoral College** which is a system of selecting **electors** who vote for the president.

Most Americans can't understand why we need an Electoral College. They ask why can't they just vote for president like they vote for every other political office. Public opinion polls show more than the great majority of Americans favor abolishing the Electoral College.

Over the past two centuries, there have been more than 700 proposals introduced in Congress to reform or eliminate the Electoral College. **More constitutional amendments have been introduced regarding the Electoral College than on any other subject, but they all failed**. After 236 years, Americans still do not get to vote for the president.

The fact is, not only is the Electoral College system nonsensical, it is **biased and unfair**. There have been several times in this country's history when the members of the Electoral College have not voted for the presidential candidate that won the popular vote.

When Americans first learn about the Electoral College system, they often find it incredible that they don't get to vote directly for the country's most important national office. The fact is, the votes cast in the hard-fought presidential elections are not actually votes for a candidate; they are actually **votes for a slate of electors**.

What many Americans *may not know* is that according to the U.S. Constitution, the electors *do not* have to vote for the candidate that won their state in the general election. In fact, when the Electoral College meets, the electors can vote for anybody they want to, even if that person is not even a candidate. **In the past, many electors have chosen not to vote for the candidate the people chose**. As stated in the U.S. Constitution, there is no restriction about who members of the Electoral College can cast their votes for.

Most people are somewhat aware that, in the United States, citizens do not get to elect presidents directly, but they think the outcome is the same as if they did. However, that is not always true. As was revealed in the 2000 presidential election, **the winner of the general election may not be the winner of the Electoral College vote**.

Well, at least Americans can take hope in the fact that the winner of the national election *usually* turns out to be the same candidate that wins the general election. In the 56 presidential elections that have been held in the United States so far, the Electoral College chose a different president than the one the people chose **only seven percent of the time**. But is that a good track record for something so important? Should the citizens of the United States be satisfied that the candidate who wins the general election *usually* gets to be president?

As we shall see, the dramatic difference in the outcome of the popular vote and the outcome of the Electoral College vote in the 2000 election was only the latest example of how the Electoral College system can go wrong, and there are strong indications it is going to happen more often in the future.

How We Got into This Mess

To understand how the strange and problematic Electoral College system of choosing presidents came about, we first have to consider the fragile political structure of our young nation as it was trying to free itself from Britain.

By 1733, thirteen British colonies had been established along the eastern seaboard of North America. They were: Connecticut, Delaware, Georgia, Maryland, Massachusetts Bay, New Hampshire, New Jersey, New York, North Carolina, Pennsylvania, Rhode Island and Providence Plantations, South Carolina, and Virginia.

To a great degree, the thirteen colonies had always been more or less self governing; therefore, there was widespread resentment whenever the British tried to impose taxes or enforce special rules that created hardships for the colonists. Over time, there were increasing protests against British rule. The most famous of the protests was the

Boston Tea Party where a group of colonists made their resentment of a recently imposed British tea tax known by dumping a large amount of British-owned tea into the Boston harbor.

In 1774, representatives of twelve of the thirteen colonies (all except Georgia) met in Philadelphia to discuss what to do about the British crackdowns that were happening in response to the protests.

In that first meeting, which became known as the **first continental congress**, the colonists could not come to an agreement about what to do about the situation. Members such as George Washington and Patrick Henry from Virginia, John Adams and Samuel Adams from Massachusetts, and John Dickinson from Pennsylvania, were not willing to take the position that the colonies should break away from British rule. They just wanted more self rule. The delegates to the congress put together a petition asking the British Parliament to address the colonists' grievances.

When the British were unwilling to agree to *any* of the colonist requests, a second congress was called to decide what to do next. This time, the meeting took on a greater sense of urgency because some militia groups in Massachusetts had already engaged British soldiers in armed conflict. Moderates among the delegates wanted to continue to try to find an accord with the British, but many of the delegates believed it was time to prepare for war. In the end, they did both. They sent another petition to Britain with a request for less taxation and more self rule, but just in case, they also began putting together an army.

The King of England refused to even read the petition. He declared the colonists rebels and sent troops to quell "the rebellion." Thus began **the Revolutionary War**.

The Articles of Confederation and the United States Constitution

After much debate, the delegates representing the thirteen colonies put together **articles of confederation** which declared the United States of America to be a confederation of sovereign states. The Articles of Confederation served as the new nation's constitution until a **constitutional convention** was convened in 1787 to lay out a governing structure. The document that came out of that convention was the **United States Constitution**.

Getting agreement as to how the new government should be organized was not an easy task. There was considerable controversy about the issue of slavery and much disagreement about how members of the governing bodies should be elected. Even after they had agreed to maintain the British concept of a two-house legislature, there was great difficulty in deciding how the two houses should be structured. Eventually, it was decided that the **House of Representatives** would be apportioned according to the population of a state. The citizens of the state would vote for their representatives, but there was much contention over how the states with smaller populations would be represented in the government. The constitutional convention was made up of delegates from **each of the states**, meaning the least populated states had as much decision-making power at the convention as the more populous states. The delegates from the smaller states felt the larger states would dominate the government.

Finally, a compromise was worked out to give the smaller states more voting power: **the senate** would be made up of two senators *appointed* from each state, no matter how large or small the population of the state was.

Of course, the big states didn't like that idea one bit, because it meant states with much smaller populations would have equal clout in the Senate. But no other solution could be agreed upon, so that method was adopted.

One major area of contention that arose regarding the apportioning of seats in the House of Representatives had to do with slaves. The Southern slave-holding states wanted to count their millions of slaves as part of their apportionment even though the slaves were not considered to be citizens of the United States. But the larger Northern states pointed out the apportionment was supposed to be based on the number of voters in a state, and of course, the slaves were not allowed to vote. There was also the issue of taxes. Because slaves were legally the property of the slave owner, the Northern states said they should be taxed as property. The Southern states disagreed, saying they were not property, but living beings. In other words, the Southern states wanted to have it both ways.

Neither side was willing to budge and it looked as if the convention would be bogged down in the issue forever.

In what would be the first of many compromises with the Southern slave states in order to get the government-making process moving again, it was decided, for purposes of representation in the House of Representatives, slaves would count as three-fifth of a person. Known as **the Three-Fifths Compromise**, it was written into the United States Constitution as follows:

> *Representatives and direct Taxes shall be apportioned among the several States which may be included within this Union, according to their respective Numbers, which shall be determined by adding to the whole Number of free Persons, including those bound to Service for a Term of Years, and excluding Indians not taxed, three-fifths of all other Persons.*

It was a decision that would have long lasting effects. It is estimated that before the Civil War, there were about nine million free whites living in the South, as compared to about four million slaves. Based on the Three-Fifths Compromise, that meant the South was given credit for an extra 2,400,000 people when the number of seats in the House of Representatives were assigned.

It meant that the Southern states not only were given disproportionate power in the Senate (two senators per state, the same number that was assigned to the much larger Northern states), but also disproportionate power in the House of Representatives. It meant that if the apportionment was based on free population, the slave states should have been apportioned 33 seats in the House of Representatives. By including their slaves and counting them as three-fifth of a person, they got 47. It also meant, they were given more electors in the Electoral College (the number of electors is based on the number of legislators as state has). As a result, for many years, Southerners dominated the Presidency, the House of Representatives, and the Supreme Court.

COMMENT:

As a direct result of giving the South disproportionate voting power, **ten of the first twelve presidents were slave holders**. The first twelve president's status with regard to slave holding is listed below:

George Washington, the first president, was a wealthy Virginia plantation owner who owned more than 200 slaves before, during, and after he was president.

The second president, **John Adams**, was from Massachusetts which was not a slave state. However, some years before he became president, he was given a slave as gift. He used her as the family cook.

Thomas Jefferson, the third president, owned a 5,000 acre plantation in Virginia and owned more than 100 slaves, including one woman, **Sally Hemings**, who was rumored to have been his mistress after his wife died. It was said she bore several of his children while he was president, all of whom, by law, remained slaves. Modern DNA evidence and analysis of the timing of his visits to his estate at Monticello seem to have proved the truth of that rumor.

James Madison, the fourth president, owned a large tobacco plantation in Virginia. He inherited hundreds of slaves and continued to hold them for the rest of his life.

James Monroe, the fifth president, was also a Virginia plantation owner and owned many slaves.

John Quincy Adams, the sixth president, being from Massachusetts was bared by state law from owning slaves.

Andrew Jackson, the seventh president, bought his first slave, a young woman, when he was only 21 years old. He later became a businessman and for a while was in the business of buying and selling slaves. At one time, he owned more than 300 slaves.

Martin Van Buren, the eighth president, was from a slave-holding family, but he personally owned only one slave.

William Henry Harrison, the ninth president, was from a Virginia plantation family that owned many slaves. Harrison was said to have illegally taken several of them with him when he traveled to states where slavery was against the law.

John Tyler, the tenth president, was also a Virginia tobacco plantation owner who owned many slaves.

James K. Polk, the eleventh president, was a slave holder from North Carolina.

Zachary Taylor, the twelfth president, was born into a slave-holding family in Virginia. Although he chose a military career, he held onto his slaves. While he was president, he held about 100 slaves.

After 1850, the rapidly increasing populations of the Northern states began to break the stranglehold the Southern states had on electing presidents. At the same time, owning slaves became much more controversial in the North. As a result, political candidates for national office, even those from Southern states, tended to transfer their slaves to a relative before running for office.

Originally, the only national office that was elected by public vote was the choosing of the states' members of the House of Representatives (and even then, only **males** were allowed to vote, and in many states, only **men who owned property could vote**).

Even the members of the U.S. Senate were selected by political leaders. The original method of **appointing senators rather than electing them**, continued to be in force until 1913 when a constitutional amendment was proposed to require direct election of senators. Many political leaders fought against the proposed amendment, and it took a year before it was finally ratified by 37 states (one more state, Delaware, ratified it in 2010). Alabama, Florida, Georgia, Kentucky, Maryland, Mississippi, Rhode Island, South Carolina, and Virginia *did not* ratify it, and Utah made a point of *explicitly rejecting* it.

However, once it was made the law of the land, even the states that didn't ratify the new constitutional amendment had to allow direct election of senators.

COMMENT:

The difficulty of getting three-fourths of the states to ratify such a common-sense concept as direct election of senators *by the citizens of their state* probably tells us how difficult it would be to get three-fourths of the states to go along with the idea of getting rid of the Electoral College system of electing presidents and vice presidents.

Dispute over How the President Should Be Chosen

Perhaps the most contentious dispute at that original **constitutional convention** in 1787 revolved around how the president was to be elected. As a result, it was one of the last issues to be resolved.

Many of the delegates felt Congress should choose the president -- or maybe even appoint a presiding **committee instead of a single president** -- but the majority of the delegates felt the people ought to be allowed to elect their president.

After much ongoing contentious debate, the mood of the convention turned away from the idea of a popular vote for president. The delegates had two reasons for deciding against a popular vote:

1) The delegates from the smaller states knew the more populous states would control the presidential elections.

2) Many of the delegates didn't trust the people to make the right decision.

The first point was true then and is still true today. Some states have much larger populations than others, and if the president was elected by popular vote, the larger-population states would have more say in who gets to be president. All of the delegates at the constitutional convention were there as representatives of individual states, and they felt their primary duty was to look out for the interests of their state. Most importantly, the smaller-population states felt they should get as much say in the election of the president as the more populous states. The only way to guarantee that was to give the smaller states *more* voting power (proportionally) than the larger states.

The second point is understandable, but less defensible. There were a lot of reasons put forward as to why the president should not be directly elected by the people, but they all came down to the same point: **the delegates at the constitutional convention did not believe the people were informed enough to make such an important decision.** While the delegates believed the people had enough information to elect their state representatives, they did not believe the people understood federal and international issues well enough to choose a national leader.

The Compromise: Electors

After much haggling, the delegates decided the people *would not* be allowed to elect the president. There would be no presidential elections. The political leaders in the states would decide who would be president and vice president by choosing **electors** who would then get together with the electors from the other states to hash out who the president and vice president would be.

After even more haggling, the delegates to the constitutional convention decided each state would be assigned **one electoral vote for each representative in the House, plus two more corresponding to each state's two senators**.

Of course, the delegates from the populous states were not happy with the idea that the smaller states would get two extra electors that had nothing to do with how many voters there were in the state. But once again, they were outvoted by the delegates from the smaller states.

COMMENT:

Today, most people probably assume the members of the Electoral College are "guided" by the outcome of their state's general election. The truth is, there is no language in the U.S. Constitution to suggest that.

At first, many states did not even bother to hold presidential elections (in the first presidential election in 1789, only 6 of the 13 original states held any sort of popular vote for president). The political leaders of each state simply decided who they wanted to be president and then sent electors to the Electoral College meeting to express those wishes.

Understandably, the people of the United States were not happy that they had no say in who their president would be. They brought political heat to bear on the politicians to allow a popular vote. Eventually all the states began to hold general elections in which the people could cast votes for their preferences for president and vice president, **even though, under the Constitution, the popular election results had no legal status** (they still don't today).

Eventually, **some** states passed laws that stated an elector could be fined if he or she did not vote for the candidate that won their state's popular vote. Nevertheless, in the 56 past presidential elections, there have been **156 instances in which an elector *did not* vote for the popular vote winner**. These electors are referred to as "**faithless electors.**" Later, I will discuss what motivated those 156 faithless electors.

To make sure the electors didn't just vote for their state's local candidate, it was written into the Constitution that the electors had to vote for at least one candidate from outside their state.

The votes of all the electors from the states would be tallied and added together, and the candidate that got the most votes would be named president. The candidate that came in second would be named vice president.

COMMENT:

Because the Constitution did not state that the electors *had to* vote for the people's choice, *it was assumed they wouldn't*, but would instead vote for whoever the leaders in the states wanted. That would result in a variety of candidates being put forward by the electors, meaning no one candidate would have the required majority and the decision would come back to the Congress. In other words, the popular vote and the Electoral College vote could both be considered to be **nominations** from which the Congress would choose a president and vice president.

But it didn't turn out that way. The Electoral College (the term "Electoral College" does not appear in the Constitution but began to appear in newspapers sometime in the early 1800s) was created at a time when political parties did not exist. When two political parties emerged in the late 1700s, the **Federalists** and the **Democratic-Republicans**, they immediately got involved in the selection of electors. It was crucial for both political parties to *try* to make sure the electors they chose were loyal **to the party** and would vote the way the party wanted them to.

Today, the two main political parties in the United States, the **Democrats** and the **Republicans**, pretty much control the election process. As a result, the election now almost always comes down to a face-off between the candidates nominated by those two parties. So far, the two major parties have been able to squeeze out any other candidates. For that reason, one of the major party candidates always wins the required absolute majority of the Electoral College votes, and therefore the decision never gets sent to the House of Representatives. If a third party candidate was to get a significant number of electoral votes, no candidate would get an absolute majority of electoral votes and the decision would be sent to the House of Representatives.

The rules of the Electoral College system can't be changed without changing the U.S. Constitution. That would require a constitutional amendment to pass both houses of congress and the approval of three-fourths of the states. Of course, that would mean the states with fewer voters would have to give up their proportional voting advantage. Most observers think that is unlikely to happen.

Another Electoral College rule was written into the Constitution to keep electors from voting for their own local friends. It says electors cannot vote for a president and vice president from the same state. Although that requirement is still in the Constitution, it has been all but forgotten (in the election of 2000, the Republican nominee for president, George Bush, and the Republican nominee for vice president, Dick Cheney, were both from Texas).

Today the electors in 48 of the 50 states (all except Maine and Nebraska) are *supposed to* (but not required to) give 100% of the electoral votes to the candidate who wins a state's popular vote. A candidate who wins the popular vote **by even a single vote margin, gets *all* of that state's electoral votes**. That means, when the Electoral College members vote, **the votes the less popular candidate received in the general election are thrown out**. It is as if those people never voted at all.

This "winner-take-all" method is not written into the Constitution, and originally only three states used that method, but in the mid 1800s, with the emergence of political parties, more states began to adopt the winner-take-all method in order to give their state more control over the election process. That decision was to shape all presidential elections to come.

After all the compromises were hashed out, each state was allotted one Electoral College member equal to the number of seats the state had in the House of Representatives. In addition, each state got two more Electoral College members to represent the state's two senators.

Below is the wording of that section as it was written into the Constitution:

> *Each State shall appoint, in such Manner as the Legislature thereof may direct, a Number of Electors, equal to the whole Number of Senators and Representatives to which the State may be entitled in the Congress: but no Senator or Representative, or Person holding an Office of Trust or Profit under the United States, shall be appointed an Elector.*

The method of selecting electors was left vague. It simply said "the states" would choose their electors and those electors would get together to choose the president and vice president.

Below is the wording of that section as it was written into the Constitution:

The Electors shall meet in their respective States, and vote by Ballot for two Persons, of whom one at least shall not be an Inhabitant of the same State with themselves. And they shall make a List of all the Persons voted for, and of the Number of Votes for each; which List they shall sign and certify, and transmit sealed to the Seat of the Government of the United States, directed to the President of the Senate. The President of the Senate shall, in the Presence of the Senate and House of Representatives, open all the Certificates, and the Votes shall then be counted. The Person having the greatest Number of Votes shall be the President, if such Number be a Majority of the whole Number of Electors appointed; and if there be more than one who have such Majority, and have an equal Number of Votes, then the House of Representatives shall immediately chuse by Ballot one of them for President; and if no Person have a Majority, then from the five highest on the List the said House shall in like Manner chuse the President. But in chusing the President, the Votes shall be taken by States, the Representation from each State having one Vote; A quorum for this Purpose shall consist of a Member or Members from two thirds of the States, and a Majority of all the States shall be necessary to a Choice. In every Case, after the Choice of the President, the Person having the greatest Number of Votes of the Electors shall be the Vice President. But if there should remain two or more who have equal Votes, the Senate shall chuse from them by Ballot the Vice President.

As you can see, there is no provision for assessing the people's wishes. It was just left up to "the states."

COMMENT:

As more states were added to the Union, the number of members in the Electoral College increased, and in 1961, a constitutional amendment (the Twenty-Third Amendment) allotted three Electoral College votes to the District of Columbia.

Today, the total number of members of the Electoral College has been permanently set at 538 (how many electors each state gets is rebalanced after every census). Half of 538 is 269. That means, to win the presidency, a candidate must win 270 Electoral College votes (the majority). As specified in the Constitution, if no candidate receives 270 votes, the decision is sent to the House of Representatives.

How Well Has the Electoral College System Worked?

In the nation's 56 past presidential elections, the Electoral College method of selecting the president has concurred with the popular vote 93% of the time.

You might ask, only 93%? Shouldn't the winner of the popular vote *always* get to be president?

Yes, but then there would be no need for the Electoral College. The truth is, as we shall see, the Electoral College system is so archaic and so flawed, it's kind of surprising it only fails seven percent of the time.

The sections that follow describe each of the U.S. presidential elections, what influenced them, and the role the Electoral College played in the outcome.

Chapter Two
Presidential Elections without Popular Elections

The Presidential Election of 1788

In the first presidential election, in 1788, **George Washington essentially ran unopposed**. He had led the country's military through the hard times of the very popular **Revolutionary War** as commander-in-chief of the **Continental Army**, and most citizens of the new country felt he deserved to be the first president. According to the new Constitution, every elector had to vote for two candidates, and they both couldn't be from the same state.

When the 1788 Electoral College ballots were cast, Washington got 69 electoral votes and John Adams got 34. Based on the Constitution's Electoral College rules, that meant Washington would be president, and Adams, the person who came in second, would be vice president.

The Presidential Election of 1792

In the second presidential election, held in 1792, Washington again ran unopposed, and again John Adams got the second most number of electoral votes (which now included electors from the two new states, Kentucky and Vermont) so they continued in office.

The Presidential Election of 1796

In the third presidential election, held in 1796, Washington chose not to run for reelection.. Therefore, there *was* contention for the office and the new concept of political parties played a big role in the election.

Vice President John Adams ran for the office as a representative of the **Federalist** Party. Former Secretary of State Thomas Jefferson and Senator Aaron Burr ran on the **Democratic-Republican** ticket.

The Federalist Party--originally the *only* American political party--believed the United States should maintain good relations with Britain and negotiated, in 1794, a treaty with Britain that became known as **the Jay Treaty**.

The Democratic-Republicans Party, on the other hand, was **a states' rights party** bent on limiting federal power. They were strongly opposed the Jay Treaty as well as most of the other Federalist policies.

The Federalists found most of their support in New England and in the larger cities, while the Democratic-Republicans found support in the rural south.

In seven of the states, Connecticut, Delaware, New Jersey, New York, Rhode Island, South Carolina, and Vermont, the electors were chosen by the state legislatures. That meant whichever party controlled a state's legislature controlled the selection of electors.

In some states, general elections were held to vote for electors after the electors said which candidate they were backing.

In four states, Kentucky, Maryland, North Carolina, and Virginia, the voters in each congressional district in the state got to vote for one elector.

Georgia and Pennsylvania held a statewide election to select electors.

Massachusetts, New Hampshire, and Tennessee used a combination of general election approaches.

The political leaders of the states were not bound by the outcome of those popular votes, but they served as a guideline as to who the people wanted.

In 1796, the vote of the Electoral College was close, with 71 votes going to Adams and 68 going to Jefferson. By rule, that meant John Adams would be president, and his opponent, Thomas Jefferson, would be vice president. It would be the only time in U.S. history that the president and the vice president came from different parties.

Chapter Three
Political Parties Evolve

The Presidential Election of 1800

Details of the 1800 presidential election read like a fictional novel of intrigue, and much of the intrigue was due to the structure of the Electoral College.

With the advent of popular voting, a few of the candidates actually campaigned. They got on their horses (literally as well as figuratively) and set out to meet the voters.

Today, we are so used to national presidential campaigning it is hard to imagine that not much national campaigning took place in the early presidential elections. Politics was something that was done in Philadelphia (the Capital at that time).

The emergence of two opposing political parties in the 1796 election set the stage for a new level of antagonism in the 1800 election. The Federalist party put up John Adams for president and Charles Pickney for vice president, while the Democratic-Republican party put up Thomas Jefferson for president and Aaron Burr for vice president.

Most of the antagonism was over the Federalist's continuing alignment with Britain and their plan to build up a centralized federal government, including the raising of an army, possibly to help Britain in its ongoing war with France.

Despite the Federalist's well-entrenched position in the seat of national power (President Washington did not belong to either party, but supported the Federalists), the Democratic-Republicans were better organized at the local level.

A long and bitter campaign for electoral votes ensued and established many of the campaigning methods we see in modern presidential elections, including the invention of **the smear campaign.**

Jefferson was philosophical about man's role in the world so the Federalists tried to paint him as against religion. They claimed God was on their side and said a vote for Adams was a vote for God and a religious presidency, while a vote for Jefferson would be a vote against God.

In this election of 1800, the Democratic-Republicans tried to paint the Federalists as against the common man and in favor of the rich and powerful (sound familiar?). They also attacked the **Alien and Sedition Acts** that had been passed by the Federalists in congress and signed by the Federalist President Adams. The acts, supposedly enacted because of a perceived threat from France made it more difficult for immigrants to become a U.S. citizen, and gave the president the power to deport immigrants if they were deemed "dangerous to the peace and safety of the United States." The acts also gave the president the power to limit freedom of speech, again if in the president's opinion such speech was "dangerous to the peace and safety of the United States." The Democratic-Republican attack on the acts was fairly successful because many citizens felt the acts went too far, especially when most people felt the chance of an attack from France was unlikely. The Democratic-Republicans said some aspects of the acts were clearly unconstitutional in that they violated the first amendment which states, "Congress shall make no law respecting an establishment of religion, or prohibiting the free exercise thereof; or abridging the freedom of speech, or of the press; or the right of the people peaceably to assemble, and to petition the Government for a redress of grievances." However, all of the members of the Supreme Court were Federalists, all appointed by Washington, so most people felt there was no chance of getting the court to overturn the acts even if they were blatantly unconstitutional.

Jefferson came right out and said the acts were created as a way to keep the Federalists in power by quashing any criticism, and in fact, the Federalists did use the acts and the threat of war to restrict what newspapers printed. They had some newspaper editors arrested and their newspapers shut down. The newspapers that were shut down were almost always publications that leaned toward the Democratic-Republicans, and this was especially important because at that time, newspapers were just beginning to play a more important role than word of mouth.

One result of the Democratic-Republican fight against the Alien and Sedition Acts was that they had considerable success in getting the newly arrived immigrants on their side, especially those from France and Ireland. It was the first election in which candidates tried to appeal to **special interest groups**.

There was also a great deal of focus on the Electoral College. Both sides saw the flaws in the Electoral College system and so they tried to manipulate those flaws to their own advantage. Both political parties also promised significant political favors to states that could swing electoral votes their way.

One or the more notable manipulation of electoral votes occurred during this 1800 election. Virginia was one of the states in which the voters **in each congressional district** voted for one elector. Thomas Jefferson realized that if his home state of Virginia would have allocated **all** of its electoral votes to him in the 1796 election, he would have been elected president. Therefore, before the 1800 election, he convinced the Virginia state legislature to change to a system in which the candidate that won the most electors, got **all** the electors. It became known as the **winner-take-all** system of allocating electoral votes.

Later, other states would realize they would have to do the same or else states that used the winner-take-all method would have more power in presidential elections. Over the next fifty years, it became the standard way of allocating electoral votes in almost all of the states (today, only Maine and Nebraska still allocate electoral votes proportionally).

In 1800, each state could choose its own election day. Therefore, the election that year went on for seven months. The last state to vote was South Carolina, and the word went out that Adams and Jefferson were tied in the Electoral College. The electors from South Carolina were solidly behind the Democratic-Republican party meaning Jefferson and Burr were going to win the national election. Therefore, a plan was hatched to have the South Carolina electors withhold one vote from Burr to make sure Jefferson would be president and Burr would come in second, making him the vice president (remember, electors had to vote for two candidates). No one knows what went wrong, but all of the South Carolina electors ended up voting for *both* Jefferson and Burr meaning the tie vote was maintained, and that meant neither candidate had a majority. As stipulated in the Electoral College section of the Constitution, the decision about who would be president was sent to the House of Representatives.

One simple solution would have been for Burr to withdraw from consideration, but he refused.

When the election of the president goes to the House of Representatives, a candidate has to get an absolute majority of the **states** (not a majority of the representatives) to be elected president. Nine of the sixteen states would have to come to an agreement.

The **lame duck** Federalists in the House of Representatives did not have enough power to swing the election their way, but they did have enough votes to keep the Democratic-Republicans from electing their candidates.

Ballot after ballot was taken with no clear winner. Days went by with no movement by either side.

At some point, the Federalists began to vote for Burr, apparently taking on an **anybody-but-Jefferson** attitude. It was clear, if this went on, nobody was going to win. It was quite possible that *there would be no president*. That presented a dire situation because the Constitution had no contingency for such an outcome (and still doesn't today).

After 34 ballots with neither side budging, everybody in Congress knew the electoral collage process was a complete failure. But because the process was mandated by the U.S. Constitution, Congress couldn't do anything about it. To change the Electoral College system, they would have to pass a bill amend the Constitution and get three-fourths of the state to ratify it. They knew the South would not give up the advantage they had in the Electoral College, so that was not a viable option.

Meanwhile, word about the stalemate in the House of Representatives was leaking out. People were upset about the whole flawed Electoral College system of electing their president. First, the people had not had any say in the election, and now their representatives in Congress seemed to be engaged in partisan squabbling that was going nowhere.

In Congress, there were rumors of armed bands of citizens marching on the capital to take things into their own hands. It was said they were coming to demand, by force of arms if need be, that Jefferson, the candidate they had voted for, be named president.

Finally, in response to what was clearly turning out to be dangerous situation, Jefferson approached the Federalist leaders and gave them assurances that he would not completely wipe out everything they had accomplished during the twelve years they had been in power. In response, in preparation for the 35th ballot, Federalist Party leader Alexander Hamilton (who strongly disliked Burr) allowed a few moderate Federalists to change their votes from Burr to Jefferson and Jefferson was elected president. Burr, having come in second, had to settle for the vice presidency.

COMMENT:

Some have speculated that the framers of the Constitution anticipated that the election of the president would often be decided by the House of Representatives, and that was what they wanted. But it seems more likely that they just hadn't considered the possibility that political parties would emerge. They couldn't have realized that political parties would complicate the presidential election process as they fought with each other for advantage.

However, the framers of the Constitution did provide a mechanism for changing it. They built in an amendment process. But they didn't want the Constitution they had so carefully crafted to be easy to change, so they stipulated that it would take agreement in Congress *and* agreement among three-fourths of the states to change it. They couldn't have realized how hard it would be to get that many states to agree on anything.

Chapter Four
Flaws in the Electoral College System

The disastrous election of 1800 started a debate in Congress about how to "fix" the Electoral College system. The debate was wide ranging and often contentious, but it was only focused on finding a solution to what had happened in the most recent election, the tie in the Electoral College that had sent the election to the House of Representatives. There was no mention of needing a popular vote, no discussion of changing how the electors were to be chosen, and no mention of electors being required by law to vote for the candidate that had won the popular vote. Despite the obvious flaws in the Electoral College system, it was clear that the politicians of that era did not want the decision about who would be president to be in the hands of the people.

The result of the congressional deliberations was a proposal to amend the Electoral College section of the Constitution. The proposed an amendment that simply stipulated that electors should make separate choices for president and vice-president.

The **Twelfth Amendment** to the Constitution was proposed by the Congress on December 9, 1803 and was ratified on June 15, 1804, just in time for the 1804 presidential election.

Below is the full text of the Twelfth Amendment:

The Electors shall meet in their respective states, and vote by ballot for President and Vice-President, one of whom, at least, shall not be an inhabitant of the same state with themselves; they shall name in their ballots the person voted for as President, and in distinct ballots the person voted for as Vice-President, and they shall make distinct lists of all persons voted for as President, and of all persons voted for as Vice-President, and of the number of votes for each, which lists they shall sign and certify, and transmit sealed to the seat of the government of the United States, directed to the President of the Senate; The President of the Senate shall, in the presence of the Senate and House of Representatives, open all the certificates and the votes shall then be counted;--The person having the greatest number of votes for President, shall be the President, if such number be a majority of the whole number of Electors appointed; and if no person have such majority, then from the persons having the highest numbers not exceeding three on the list of those voted for as President, the House of Representatives shall choose immediately, by ballot, the President. But in choosing the President, the votes shall be taken by states, the representation from each state having one vote; a quorum for this purpose shall consist of a member or members from two-thirds of the states, and a majority of all the states shall be necessary to a choice.... The person having the greatest number of votes as Vice-President, shall be the Vice-President, if such number be a majority of the whole number of Electors appointed, and if no person have a majority, then from the two highest numbers on the list, the Senate shall choose the Vice-President; a quorum for the purpose shall consist of two-thirds of the whole number of senators, and a majority of the whole number shall be necessary to a choice. But no person constitutionally ineligible to the office of President shall be eligible to that of Vice-President to the United States.

Notice that the Twelfth Amendment made few changes to the original language regarding how the president and vice president are chosen. It still *does not* say, or *even suggest*, that electors should vote for the winner of the popular vote. In fact, **it still doesn't even suggest there needs to be a popular vote.**

COMMENT:

When the first few presidents were chosen, only a few states held general elections. The decision about who would be president was pretty much up to the political leaders in the states. Then they selected electors who would vote that way.

Although Americans now take the election of a president very seriously, voting for the president in an public election is not even mentioned in the Constitution. However, some states (not all) have passed laws that say the members of the state's slate of electors **have to** vote for the winner of that state's general presidential election. However, the most the state can do is levy a fine on an elector who disobeys that *suggestion.* (Some legal scholars say such laws are unconstitutional because there is nothing in the Electoral College section of the U.S. Constitution that says an elector has to vote in any specified way.) There is much ado about today's presidential elections, and untold amounts of money are spent on trying to get Americans to vote for one candidate or another, the results of that voting have no legal status. No matter who the citizens of the country vote for, members of the Electoral College can vote for anybody they want to (and as we shall see later, many have ignored the popular vote and done just that).

As a result of the Twelfth Amendment, in the presidential elections that followed, the members of the Electoral College chose presidents and vice presidents from the same party.

However, little else changed. It was still the Electoral College that chose the president and vice president, and five states still refused to allow the voters to have anything to do with choosing the electors.

Many of today's politician still do not want the people to be able to vote to elect the president directly. The reason is that whichever political party controls the smaller-population states still has much to gain by keeping the Electoral College system as it is.

Over the years, the Electoral College system has sometimes failed to agree with the people's choice for president. So why haven't the people risen up to demand an end to the Electoral College? Hard to say. It's probably just because we tend to forget about things if they seem to be working "all right." Only when things go wrong, do we get riled up and want to do something about it.

COMMENT:

The presidential elections of 1796 and 1800, the young nation's first nationally contested elections, revealed **the flaws in the Electoral College system.**

The most serious flaws are:

1. Electors are not chosen by the people. There is nothing in the Electoral College section of the Constitution that says the electors have to be guided by the popular vote for president and vice president. In fact, there is nothing in the Constitution at all about the need for a general election by the people. It simply says "the states" will select the electors.

2. Electors are not required to vote for the candidates chosen by the people. Under the Constitution, electors are not required to vote for the candidates chosen by the people's vote. That means electors can, and sometimes do, vote for their own preferred candidate instead of voting for the candidate preferred by the political party that named them as electors (see the later section on "faithless electors").

3. The current Electoral College winner-take-all system may influence how people vote. Because of the winner-take-all system, if the pre-election polls show that most of the voters in a state are clearly planning to vote for one candidate, there is little point for people to vote for a different candidate. That makes it less likely people will bother to vote at all. (Modern sophisticated polling methods have gotten much better at predicting which candidate will win a state.) If the polls show a lopsided victory is all but assured, **what is the point of anybody voting for either side?**

For example, in every election for the past sixty years (except for 1964 when Johnson won the national vote overwhelmingly), the Republican candidate for president has won the winner-take-all electoral votes in Idaho, Montana, North Dakota, South Dakota, Utah, and Wyoming. So, with the polls already clearly showing that trend will continue in the 2012 presidential election, what is the point of *anybody* voting for president in those states? A vote for the Republican candidate is pointless because everybody knows the Republican always wins. And a vote for the Democratic candidate is also pointless because when the Electoral College meets to do the actual vote for president, under the winner-take-all system, **those votes will be thrown out.** It will be as if those people never voted at all.

4. A viable third party candidate can change the outcome. In the presidential election of 2000, most people believe third-party candidate Ralph Nader took enough votes away from Al Gore to cost him the presidency. Under the Electoral College system, it's surprising that hasn't happened more often.

5. A viable third party candidate could send the decision about who becomes president to the House of Representatives. According to the U.S. Constitution, a candidate has to get an **absolute majority** of all electoral votes to win the presidency. In a close election, if a third party candidate gets some Electoral College votes, it would make it hard for any candidate to get an absolute majority. In that case, the decision about who would be the president would go to the House of Representatives, and whichever party happens to be in the majority in the House at that time will undoubtedly determine which candidate gets to be president, no matter how the people voted. In the past, third party candidates *have* gained some Electoral College votes, but those elections were not close. It seems likely that sooner or later, a strong third party candidate will throw the election to the House of Representatives.

6. States with smaller populations have proportionally more electors than states with larger populations. Because even the smallest states are guaranteed under the Constitution to get at least three electoral votes, those states have a greater say in who will get to be president and vice president.

Because the design of the Electoral College gives more electoral voting power to the smaller-population states, a vote for president by a Wyoming resident counts about four times more than a vote by a California resident. That advantage was critical in the presidential election of 2000. In that election, **Al Gore won the 2000 presidential general election by 543,895 votes.** He did it by winning states with large populations, but the states with smaller populations, added together, had more Electoral College votes. As a result, Gore didn't get to be president despite winning the popular vote by a comfortable margin. It was the fourth time in U.S. history in which the candidate that won the popular vote didn't get to be president.

As you might expect, after the drawn-out battle in the House of Representatives with Burr refusing to cooperate, Aaron Burr was no longer looked on as favorably by the Democratic-Republicans. As a result, he was given little to do during his four-year reign as vice president.

When Jefferson ran for reelection in 1804, he dumped Burr in favor of New York Governor George Clinton.

The presidential campaign of 1800 saw, for the first time, **inflammatory, personal attacks** on the good names of the candidates. Personal attacks were not taken as lightly back then as they are now, and as a result, they **often resulted in duels.** After the 1800 election, a series of letters were circulated accusing Aaron Burr of various despicable acts. Thomas Jefferson, who was planning to run for reelection, replaced Burr with Governor **George Clinton** of New York to be his running mate.

As a result, Burr declared himself a candidate for governor of New York. Alexander Hamilton, the former Secretary of the Treasury, campaigned aggressively against Burr and Burr was defeated.

The insults continued even after the election until eventually, **Burr challenged Hamilton to a duel** and Hamilton accepted. On the morning of July 11, 1804, while Burr was still finishing out his term as vice president, the dueling parties were take by boat to New Jersey to avoid the anti-duel laws of New York state. There is disagreement about exactly what happened because everyone present was instructed to turn away before shots were fired (so they could not be brought into court to testify as to what happened). What is not in dispute is that Burr killed Hamilton with one shot.

Burr was never prosecuted for the killing.

Chapter Five
Presidential Politics Evolves

The Presidential Election of 1804

Although there was trouble brewing in Europe at the time of the presidential election of 1804, it was a period of relative peace in the United States. The American shipping trade had been further developed under President Jefferson, which resulted in an improved economy, and his successful negotiation and completion of the Louisiana Purchase was widely seen as a great achievement.

Therefore, Jefferson, with this new vice-presidential candidate, George Clinton, was elected over **Charles Cotesworth Pinckney**, a Federalist from South Carolina.

COMMENT:

In 1803, President Thomas Jefferson initiated a deal with France to purchase a huge tract of land that became known as **the Louisiana Purchase**.

Jefferson was not sure at first whether or not he had the legal power to purchase land from a foreign government. However, he eventually decided it would be the best way to protect the port of New Orleans through which a great deal of the nation's farm produce passed.

Jefferson had previously served as Ambassador to France, and he had a tenuous working relationship with France. After Spain transferred *some* of the territory west of the Mississippi to France, Jefferson undertook to buy land from France in and around New Orleans.

Napoleon knew that his ongoing conflicts with Britain would eventually lead to war, so he needed all the money he could get. Therefore, he proposed to sell **all** of France's land west of the Mississippi to the United States for the total sum of 15 million dollars (about 3 cents an acre).

There was resistance in Congress over the deal, but the Southern states favored it as long as Jefferson, a slave holder, agreed to allow the institution of slavery to expand into the new territory.

Eventually, the deal was made and the United States transferred three million in gold to France as a down payment and issued bonds for the other twelve million.

The U.S. assumed the new land stretched from the Gulf of Mexico in the south and into Canada to the north and all the way from the Mississippi River to the Rocky Mountains.

Spain disputed the sale and continued to claim the land.

When Jefferson funded the Lewis and Clark expedition to map the new territory, Spain sent troops to try to stop them. But they could never find the Lewis and Clark party.

Following river routes and being guided by friendly Indians, Lewis and Clark eventually made it all the way to the West Coast near what is now Portland, Oregon.

With the threat from Spain still looming, Jefferson established forts in several places to secure the new territory.

The new lands were to play a key role in three future conflicts, the Indian Wars, the War of 1812, and the Civil War.

The Presidential Election of 1808

In 1808, after the successful presidency of Thomas Jefferson, there was little doubt that his Secretary of State, James Madison, would be elected over Federalist Charles C. Pinckney who was running for president for the second time.

George Clinton was elected as his vice president. He was the first person to serve as vice president under two different presidents.

The Presidential Election of 1812

During the early part of the 19th century, the Democratic-Republican party was as dominant in U.S. politics as the Federalist had been in the first few presidential elections. And because the South continued to vote as a block, the Democratic-Republican presidential candidates were always slave holders from Virginia. With the support of *all* the Southern states, they always won easily.

In the election of 1812, they nominated **James Madison** for reelection. He chose **Elbridge Gerry**, the former governor of Massachusetts as his running mate.

The Federalists, desperate for a win, supported a dissident Democratic-Republican, **DeWitt Clinton**.

The campaign election was, as usual, mostly about the issue of slavery, but this time there was also a war going on. Early in the election campaign, the United States declared war on Britain. It became known as the War of 1812.

The war was popular and as American have a history of reelecting presidents when a war is under way, they overwhelmingly voted to give Madison a second term.

COMMENT:

The war of 1812, like all wars, changed the political landscape and influenced several of the presidential elections that were to follow. The war started as an outgrowth (some said a sideshow) of ongoing battles between two great military powers of that era, Britain and France. Much of their war was being fought on the high seas, and when Britain tried to blockade France, trade ships from the United States sometimes got caught up in the conflict.

In the early 1800s Napoleon Bonaparte was running roughshod over Europe, but Britain ruled the seas. Britain put together an alliance of countries against Bonaparte's France, and in the early months of 1812, they began to capture American trade ships. Britain claimed the trade ships were helping the French, if only to re-supply France with needed goods. The American trade ships were taken as the spoils of war, and the captured sailors were forced to serve on British warships.

In response, on the first day of June in 1812, the United States shocked the world by declaring war on Britain. It was a reaction not only to the taking of American ships, but also a reaction to a perceived violation of America's neutrality in the European conflict. President Madison declared Britain's actions were an affront to America's honor.

Although America's declaration of war on Britain surprised many people throughout the world, the U.S. had some ongoing unsettled issues with Britain that played a part in it. For one thing, Britain had been trying to thwart the American expansion into American western territories the British wanted for themselves. They were arming the western Indians, trying to get them to organize against the United States.

In addition, there were many in the U.S. government that hoped not only to expand into the West, but also into Canada. Toward that end, one of the first American acts in the war was to invade Canada. American forces under General Hull, the governor of Michigan territory, invaded Canada north of Detroit. However, the attack was not well coordinated and the British not only easily repelled it, but in response attacked Detroit. Within a month, General Hull was forced to surrender Detroit to the British.

Several sea battles ensued, with American ships faring surprisingly well, but the land battles did not go so well. When De Witt Clinton, the governor of New York, sent troops into Canada near Niagara Falls, they were soon forced back and became trapped at the edge of the Niagara River with no way to cross back into the United States. Three hundred Americans were killed and nearly a thousand were taken prisoner.

Although the war wasn't going so well for the Americans, the people were mostly behind Madison and being patriotic in defiance of other, more powerful countries, was held in high regard. In fact, the American national anthem, **The Star-Spangled Banner,** was written during the war of 1812 (many Americans mistakenly believe it was written during the Revolutionary War). The song's lyrics came from a poem titled "Defence of Fort

McHenry" written by a 35-year-old lawyer named Francis Scott Key. He wrote the poem soon after he witnessed the British 25-hour bombardment of Fort McHenry, a large fort built in 1798 to defend Baltimore Harbor. At the time, the poem was sung to the tune of a British song written for a men's social club in London. With that tune more or less intact, it was named the national anthem 117 years later, in 1913.

In the War of 1812, even pirates played a role. Realizing that the U.S. was outmatched in naval power, the U.S. government offered to commission any armed vessel that was willing to help, even pirate vessels.

The famous pirate, Jean Lafitte, had been operating several smuggling ships out of New Orleans and had only recently been forced to retreat to an out-of-the-way bay further south.

A few months after the U.S. declared war on Britain, the British sent a delegation to try to recruit Lafitte to their side. They offered Lafitte and his men British citizenship and land in British areas of the western part of North America if they would fight against the Americans. Lafitte was a good enough tactician to see that the Americans held the land and therefore the advantage. He turned down the offer (and surprisingly didn't kill the envoys).

When the British mounted an offensive against New Orleans, Andrew Jackson brought troops to repel them.

The city was in dire straits and Jackson was outnumbered. He had only two ships and a few thousand unseasoned troops. When he learned Lafitte had many ships and seasoned fighting men, Jackson approached him with a deal: if the pirates would help defend the city, Jackson promised them full pardons. After the pirate agreed, Jackson managed to convince the Louisiana legislature to make the pardons official.

It is said that Lafitte's trained fighting men, and the pirates' knowledge of the area, were instrumental in the defense of the New Orleans. (By the way, just to make sure everyone knew he was still a pirate at heart, Lafitte went back to pirating after the war was over.)

After Napoleon's infamous failure to invade and hold Russia (he invaded Russia with 400,000 troops but came back with only

40,000), several countries united against France, and by 1814 Napoleon was defeated. Britain and France signed a peace treaty, and that put an end to the issues that had led to the War of 1812. The United States and Britain decided to call it a stalemate, and the two countries signed **the Treaty of Ghent** on the day before Christmas, 1814.

However, the treaty was signed in Europe and as a result, the news that the war was over had to come to America by ship. And even after the news of the treaty had reached the East Coast, given the lack of rapid communications during that era, especially in the West, the news took over two months to reach all the troops that were still fighting. The last major battle of the war, a British victory at the second Battle of Fort Bowyer at Mobile Bay, Alabama, took place on February 11, 1815.

Although the war was a stalemate with no territorial gains or losses, it did bring about a feeling of national pride and unity. And when the U.S. attempts to annex Canada ended, it also marked the beginning of the **"era of good feelings"** between the U.S. and Britain.

The Presidential Election of 1816

By **1816**, the Federalists had all but given up hope. They didn't even nominate a candidate, and Democratic-Republican James Monroe, another Virginian, won easily. The only contention was whether the electoral votes of the new state of Indiana should be counted. For some reason, Representative John W. Taylor of New York objected to including Indiana's electoral votes. He was voted down and the votes of Indiana *were* counted (and it changed nothing).

The Presidential Election of 1820

By **the election of 1820**, the Federalist party was no more. Democratic-Republican **James Monroe ran for reelection unopposed**. It would be the last time any candidate was to run for president unopposed.

After the War of 1812, politics in the early 1800s seemed relatively calm. There were ongoing troubles with the Indians as more and more western lands were developed, either pushing the Indians farther west or onto reservations.

In the West, continuing controversy over the issue of slavery was dividing the people. More and more people of the United States were saying slavery was not only inhuman, but it was also unconstitutional. America, they said, was supposed to be the land of the free, and yet slavery was still the law of the land in a time when many other countries were outlawing it.

France had abolished slavery until Napoleon brought it back temporarily by enslaving the citizens of the countries he invaded.

Countries such as Russia and other eastern European countries had abolished slavery many years before in the late 1700s.

Denmark and Norway abolished slavery and the slave trade.

In 1807, the British not only abolished slavery, but their ships began stopping slave ships and arresting their captains. It is estimated that the British anti-slave operation freed more than 150,000 captured Africans.

American's neighbors, Canada and Mexico had either abolished slavery or were in the process of doing it district by district.

The constant contention over the issue of slavery continued as the nation expanded westward. The Southern states tried to enact laws that made slavery of African-Americans legal in any new western state that wanted to join the Union. The Northern states fought against it.

The **Missouri Compromise** of 1821 maintained the balance of slave states and free states, which meant slavery would not be as big an issue in the upcoming elections as many had feared.

Chapter Six
The Politics of Slavery

Dissonance over the issue of slavery had been brewing in the United States since the country declared its independence from Britain. In the early 1800s, it became the predominant issue in presidential politics.

Many Northerners were outraged at the very idea of slavery, saying it was contrary to the United States Bill of Rights. Those in favor of slavery pointed out that there was no mention of slavery in the U.S. Constitution (which is true; many of the framers of the Constitution, including George Washington, John Adams, Thomas Jefferson, and James Madison were slave owners and they were careful to never use the word "slave" anywhere in the Constitution).

Whenever new states petitioned to join the United States, it brought the issue to a head. The Southern slave states feared if new states were allowed to join the Union as free states, the shift of power in Congress might lead to the eventual outlawing of slavery altogether. As a result, the slave states used their power in the Senate to keep new states from joining the Union unless they agreed to allow slavery.

The situation came to a head when Missouri wanted to join the United States. Missouri was the first state to be created out of the Louisiana purchase, and most of the region's citizens had come from the South. Therefore, there was an assumption that it would be a slave state. A House of Representatives committee approved Missouri's petition to become a state in 1819, but James Tallmadge of New York added an amendment specifying Missouri had to be a free state. Furthermore, his amendment stated that the new state would be prohibited from importing slaves and that all current slaves that had been born in the region had to be freed when they reached the age of 25. The bill was passed by the House on February 17, 1819.

Of course, the Southern slave states used their disproportionate power in the Senate to vote it down.

After much contentious debate, as so often happens in politics, a compromise was reached and the bill was passed. The compromise was that the northern part of Massachusetts would break off to become a new state (Maine), and it would be admitted to the Union as a free state, and at the same time, Missouri would be admitted as a slave state. That way, there would be twelve slave states represented in the Senate which would make sure the twelve Northern free states couldn't pass any anti-slave legislation. The law also included a stipulation that slavery should not be allowed in any territory north of latitude 36° 30' North (which marked the northern border of Missouri). The law became known as **the Missouri Compromise**.

As is typical of such compromises, neither side was happy with it. Thomas Jefferson said the division of the country created by **the Compromise Line** would eventually lead to the destruction of the Union. John Randolph, a Virginia slave owner himself, denounced the compromise and called Henry Clay, the Speaker of the House, "the great compromiser" (not a complimentary term). He sent plenty of other insults Clay's way, and not surprisingly, soon thereafter, the two met to fight a duel. Although shots reportedly were fired, the word from the dueling ground came back that the only injury was to Randolph's clothes (in other words, Clay did fire at Randolph, but it was a near miss).

Regardless of how Randolph felt about slavery, he felt all governing power should be in the hands of the states. He thought states ought to be free to accept or reject federal laws.

It is interesting to note that despite being a slave owner all his life, Randolph wrote a will that decreed all his slaves should be freed upon his death. Known as **manumission**, the practice of specifying the freeing of slaves in a will was becoming more common as the debate about slavery heated up, and Thomas Jefferson also specified in his will that his slaves be freed.

Later in life, Randolph said he regretted ever having owned slaves and his will provided money to be used to resettle his slaves in the free state of Ohio. After he died, three hundred and eighty three of Randolph's former slaves accepted the offer. However, at that time, racism was as rampant in Ohio as it was most everywhere else in this country, so when they arrived, they were met by mobs of angry white men with guns who drove them further on west. Sadly, the Ohio land that had been paid for with money from Randolph's will had already been sold off to white men, and the sellers had run off with the money. No Ohio law enforcement officials were willing to do anything about it, so all the "**Randolph slaves**" could do was move on. Eventually, many of them were employed by Quakers sympathetic to their plight, and the rest either found employment doing odd jobs in the few Ohio counties that would accept them, or else they moved on west and disappeared.

The Presidential Election of 1824

The presidential election of 1824 turned out to be as contentious as the battles in Congress over slavery. It was to be the **first election in which the candidate that won the most votes--both popular and in the Electoral College--did not get to be president.**

As I noted earlier, after the demise of the Federalist party, the Democratic-Republican Party much had things their own way. In every presidential election since 1796, the winner had been a member of the Democratic-Republican Party.

But by 1824, the people of the country were becoming disillusioned with the brand of "**insider politics**" that was becoming the norm, and that disillusionment was soon to have a devastating effect on the Democratic-Republican party's grip on political power.

Following the established precedent of serving only two terms, President Monroe chose not to run for reelection in 1824. He said he was ready to retire to his estate at Monroe Hill near Charlottesville, Virginia (his estate is now part of the campus of the University of Virginia).

As a result, **the 1824 election season** began, just as it had for all prior elections since the demise of the Federalist Party, with a **Democratic-Republican Congressional nominating caucus** (known then as the "**King Caucus**") being held to decide who would be the next president and vice president. For president, they selected a

Southern slave holder, **William Harris Crawford** of Georgia, and for vice president, they selected **Albert Gallatin** of Pennsylvania.

COMMENT:

The official **Democratic-Republican candidates, Crawford and Gallatin** were not well known at the time of their nomination. Nevertheless, both of them had been in and around politics for much of their adult lives.

In 1803, Crawford was elected to the Georgia House of Representatives, and in 1807 he was appointed to the U.S. Senate by the Georgia legislature (remember, until 1913, U.S. senators were not elected by the people but were appointed by state legislatures). In 1813, President James Madison had appointed Crawford to serve as minister to France. He served in that post until the end of the War of 1812, and when he returned from France, Madison appointed him Secretary of War, and then later Secretary of the Treasury. He remained in the latter position until, despite serious health problems, he was nominated to be a candidate for president by the Democratic-Republican congressional caucus.

Albert Gallatin's story is a more complex and interesting one. Born into a wealthy and influential family in Switzerland, he studied at the elite Academy of Geneva where he discovered the philosophy of Jean-Jacques Rousseau and Physiocracy (the belief that the wealth of nations is based on the land and agriculture).

In 1880, at age 19, he began hearing about the democracy movement in the new country across the seas known as the United States. Like many other young Europeans, he was fascinated with the new democratic county and soon set out to see it for himself.

In America, he tried various business ventures without much success, so he had to make his living teaching French. Eventually, he was able to use his family's influence to get a position at Harvard College. That didn't last long. He again set out to make his fortune in various businesses from farming to retailing to glass making. At one point, in response to the perceived threat from France, the Commonwealth of Pennsylvania called out to its militia and Gallatin signed a contract to make muskets for them. That didn't turn out to be very profitable either.

But Gallatin had always had an interest in politics, and in 1793, he lobbied for an appointment to the U.S. Senate, aligning himself with the Democratic-Republicans and against the Federalists.

He was appointed to the Senate, but the Federalists protested his appointment, saying he had not been a citizen of the United States for a long enough period to be a senator.

It went to a vote, and the Federalists used their voting power to remove him from the Senate. But he did not go without at fight, and it was his battle to stay in the Senate and his impassioned oratory that brought him some attention, especially from the anti-Federalist forces. (One outcome of his battle to stay in the Senate was that the proceedings of the Senate, for the first time, had to be made public.)

Back home in Pennsylvania, he played a role in the Whiskey Rebellion, a protest against a new tax on whiskey that grew violent. When the government sent in the Army to put down the protest, Gallatin used his notoriety and his skillful oratory to calm the situation.

As a result, he was elected to House of Representatives in 1795 where he became an anti-Federalist leader of the Democratic-Republicans. From then on, he held various positions in the government until 1824 when he was nominated to be a candidate for vice president by the Democratic-Republican congressional caucus.

With the people crying out for more open politics, some politicians in the Democratic-Republican party saw opportunity. Many decided against participating in the "king making" party caucus. As a result, to the great surprise of the party leaders, only 66 of the party's 231 members showed up.

The caucus went ahead and nominated Crawford and Gallatin, but the lack of party participation was a sign of things to come.

Soon after the "official" Democratic-Republican caucus had nominated Crawford and Gallatin, three other Democratic-

Republicans, **John Quincy Adams**, **Henry Clay**, and **Andrew Jackson** defied the party leaders and made it known *they* wanted to be president.

COMMENT:

The other Democratic-Republican candidates, John Quincy Adams, Henry Clay, and Andrew Jackson were better known. Adams was the son of the former president. Reportedly, he suffered from depression and was unsure of himself and not all that interested in politics. Nevertheless, he followed in his father's footsteps by serving as a foreign minister in several European countries.

Upon his return, he was still not sure he wanted to get involved in politics, but friends of his father pushed him in that direction. In 1802, he was elected to the Massachusetts State Senate.

That same year, he ran as the Federalist candidate for the United States House of Representatives, but he lost. Nevertheless, the Federalists soon got him appointed to the U.S. Senate where he served until 1808. As a senator, he angered the Federalists who had appointed him by supporting the Louisiana Purchase which they were against.

The Federalists, who controlled the Massachusetts legislature, decided to replace him. In response, Adams became a Democrat-Republican.

When James Madison, a Democratic-Republican, was elected president, he appointed Adams as foreign minister to Russia. He was accompanied in Saint Petersburg by his wife Louisa, and it was said at the time she made up for his lack of charm in social situations, and in fact, she soon became a favorite invitee at the tsar's parties.

By 1818, Adams was back in the U.S. serving as Secretary of State in the cabinet of Democratic-Republican President James Monroe.

With the election of 1824 drawing near, and it looking more and more like the election was going to be wide open, the New England Democratic-Republican party went looking for a "favorite son" candidate. Their choice fell to Adams, and eventually he was forced to accept their nomination.

Henry Clay was from a Virginian family who owned a large number of slaves. But Henry was not interested in the life of the plantation owner and instead decided to become a lawyer even though he had no formal education in the law. To learn about the law he secured an appointment as an assistant to the Virginia State Attorney where he learned about courtroom proceedings *and* about politics.

In 1797, he moved to Kentucky to practice law on his own. In Kentucky, everyone agreed he had a knack for politics and oratory, and in 1803, he was elected to the Kentucky General Assembly. It wasn't long before he was appointed by the Kentucky legislature to the U.S. Senate even though he was only 29 years old (the Constitution requires U.S. senators to be over the age of thirty). No one seemed to notice, or if they did, they didn't care.

In 1807, Clay returned to Kentucky where he was soon elected Speaker of the Kentucky House of Representatives.

However, his aggressive approach to lawmaking angered several members of the legislature, and he was involved in some scuffles on the floor of the House. One such scuffle resulted in Clay challenging a legislator named Humphrey Marshall to a duel. The rules of the duel were that each man would get three shots. One of Clay's shots grazed Marshall's chest, and one of Marshall's shots hit Clay in the thigh. Both men survived and honor was served.

In 1810, the Kentucky state legislature again appointed Clay to the U.S. Senate. But one year later, he was elected to the U.S. House of Representatives.

Such was his reputation that he was elected Speaker of the House on the first day in office. Thereafter, he was re-elected five times to the House and each time he was reelected as Speaker of the House. It is important to note that Clay completely changed the role of the Speaker of the House from parliamentarian (merely a keeper of the rules) to political leader. He was the first U.S. Speaker of the House to appoint his allies to key committee chairmanships as a way of controlling what became law and what did not. He also used his position to support hostilities against Britain which, in time, turned into the War of 1812.

By 1812, Clay was becoming quite prosperous and owned a 600-acre tobacco and hemp plantation and 60 slaves of his own.

In 1816, he became president of the **American Colonization Society**, a group that wanted to send free blacks back to Africa. Under Clay's leadership, the group founded a colony in Africa called Monrovia. Clay said the god of nature had decreed against the amalgamation of the black and white races as proven by the obvious differences of skin color and physical constitution. The main purpose of the group was to deport free blacks because they posed a threat to the practice of slavery, but some abolitionists from the North also got behind the effort.

As the election of 1824 loomed, it became clear the Democratic-Republican caucus's nomination of Crawford and Gallatin was not receiving wide support, and Clay made his bid for the presidency.

Andrew Jackson was the first candidate for president that could be described as **an outsider**. Although he was, like Clay, a Southerner who owned slaves, he was not part of the Southeast Coast group of political insiders. He was from Tennessee.

Little is known about Jackson's childhood except that his father died before he was born, His father and his two brothers all died in the Revolutionary War.

When Jackson was thirteen, he joined up with a local militia to fight in the Revolutionary War. They made him a courier, but he was soon captured by the British and held as a prisoner of war. He was mistreated, almost starved to death, and contracted smallpox, leaving him with a lifelong hatred of the British. Soon after his release, his mother died, leaving him an orphan at the age of fourteen.

After that, he was bounced around between relatives, had little education, and worked at various odd jobs. Eventually, he went to North Carolina to study law. Not all that much is known about his studies or his early law career, but he was said to have practiced law in the western part of North Carolina, the area that was to become the state of Tennessee.

When Tennessee became a state in 1796, he was elected as its first representative in Congress. Meanwhile, he was growing wealthy from investments and from his law practice. He bought up huge tracks of land in Tennessee, and eventually accrued 150 slaves.

He also became an active member of the Tennessee militia. During the War of 1812, several Indian tribes banded together, and with the aid of the British, attacked western towns. Jackson took his Tennessee militia into battle against them, and the Indians were repelled. Jackson's rank was raised to major general, and he started to get a national reputation as a capable military leader.

In 1814, when New Orleans came under British attack, Jackson took over command of the region's defense. Many others came to join the defense effort, including Davy Crockett and Sam Houston, and by the beginning of 1815, the British were routed.

During that conflict, Jackson became widely known as a tough and very strict officer. The word got out that his men called him "Old Hickory" (tough as old hickory wood), and the nickname stuck.

By the end of the War of 1812, Jackson was being described as a national hero. He received an official gold medal of thanks from the U.S. Congress, and more than a few political leaders began thinking of him as a potential political candidate. In 1823, the Tennessee legislature appointed him U.S. senator and encouraged him to run for president in the presidential election of 1824.

As the 1824 campaign progressed, it started to become clear that William Crawford, the Democratic-Republican party's official choice for president, was not fairing well in the pubic eye. The campaigning had hardly begun when Crawford suffered a stroke that was said to have been brought on by an overdose of prescribed medication. He recovered well, but it hampered his ability to campaign and gave people doubts about his overall health.

It was only the first of many setbacks faced by the Democratic-Republican party leaders. Adams, the son of the nation's second president, who had formerly been a Federalist, was clearly gathering support from the old Federalists in the Northeast, and Jackson was beginning to look like the people's choice in the South and in the West.

Of the two, the party leaders thought Jackson would be the easiest to discredit. They published many articles in Democratic-Republican newspapers that said Jackson had **no real national political experience,** that he was **nothing but a frontier backwoodsman.**

But that didn't work very well because it made the people think of Jackson as "one of them."

Then the Adams backers **said Jackson was a murderer.** They said they had proof that he had executed captured Indians without a trial and had even executed captured British troops. There may have been some truth to those charges, but many people saw those incidents as just part of war, and Andrew Jackson had been, after all, a military hero in Florida and in the War of 1812.

As a last resort, Jackson's political opponents said he had killed men in unfair duels, and that he was an adulterer living with another man's wife.

Although there was some truth to those charges as well, Jackson's support among the "common men" in the West and the South never wavered. In that era, although adultery was a serious matter and did hurt Jackson's reputation, duels were seen as matter of honor between gentlemen.

COMMENT:

Although killing a man in a duel these days would certainly hurt a presidential candidate's chances of winning an election, it might well have been a political advantage in Jackson's time.

Jackson was rumored to have killed many men in duels, and it was a sign of the times that he never disputed the charge. His reputation of having great prowess with a pistol made a lot of the men of that era look up to him (and remember, at that time, only men could vote).

However, had the real truth about his dueling history been known at the time, it would have been considerably less flattering. While it was true that he was hot tempered and quick to challenge a man to a duel, the fact is his duels usually didn't take place. The problem was that he had a habit of challenging men to duels in the heat of the moment, only to find out later that his prospective opponent was a skillful and experienced duelist.

For example, at the tender age of 21, Jackson was trying to learn how to practice law. In one of his first court cases, an experienced lawyer ridiculed Jackson's judicial knowledge. Jackson immediately challenged the man to a duel. The duel was scheduled, but in the meantime, Jackson had learned more about the man's reputation as a duelist and had second thoughts. The details are lost to time, but the outcome on the field of honor was that both agreed to fire into the air.

Over the next several years, other duels were offered, but never took place. Not, that is until Jackson made an enemy of the governor of Tennessee, John Sevier. The story is that the two feuded for years until a duel was finally scheduled. However, before the day of the scheduled duel, they happened to meet on the trail. In a scene right out of one of that era's notorious Western "dime novels," Jackson dismounted and pulled out his pistol. Sevier dismounted and drew his sword. Quite a few insults were exchanged before they both got back on their horses and went on their way. For some reason, the scheduled duel never happened.

The one duel that did happen, was indeed a deadly one. It was again a feud between lawyers, but it came to a head in a bar fight. After the fisticuffs, Jackson challenged a young lawyer named Charles Dickinson to a duel. The duel took place at Harrison's Mill, Kentucky. Unfortunately for Jackson, the young man turned out to be quite a good marksman, and when the command to fire was given, the young man shot Jackson square in the chest. Jackson managed to stay on his feet and shot Dickinson in the stomach, killing him. Jackson survived, but he was to carry Dickinson's bullet in his chest for the rest of his life.

The attacks on John Quincy Adams by Jackson's supporters were quite different. They said Adams was out of touch with the people. They called him an **Eastern elitist**, possibly, he was even a secret royalist. They constantly brought up Adams former involvement with the Federalists.

Those kinds of attacks were not likely to erode Adams's support in the Northeast and in the urban areas of the country, but they did hurt him with the voters Jackson was reaching out to, the so-called "common man" (and there were a lot more of them).

Meanwhile, one of the best known candidates for president, Henry Clay, was getting left behind. Although he was a well-known politician, it was clear he was not popular among the people. He could only count on his home state of Kentucky, and maybe some additional support from the two neighboring states.

Jackson won both the popular vote and the electoral vote. He racked up overwhelming victories in Alabama, Indiana, Mississippi, North Carolina, Pennsylvania, and Tennessee.

Adams won the popular vote in the Northeast states, Connecticut, Maine, Massachusetts, New Hampshire, and Rhode Island

The nation was divided by region: Jackson won the rural states by large margins, but Adams won the more populous states of the Northeast.

The only two states Crawford won were Delaware and Georgia. However, that doesn't mean Crawford was the people's choice in those two states. Delaware and Georgia did not allow a popular vote. The electors were chosen by the legislature. They were Democratic-Republican party loyalists who did their duty and cast their Electoral College votes for whoever the party leaders told them to -- in this case, Crawford.

The final Electoral College vote was Jackson 99, Adams 84, Crawford 41, Clay 37.

Since no candidate had the required absolute majority of 131 electoral votes, the selection of the president would once again have to go to the U.S. House of Representatives. And as stated in the Twelfth Amendment, the House would have to choose from the top three candidates.

Interestingly, the vice president *was* elected. John Calhoun of South Carolina won the majority of votes for vice president and therefore was elected to that office no matter which of the presidential candidates won.

COMMENT:

Because **Henry Clay** had come in fourth in the Electoral College voting, he was eliminated from consideration. However, he was still the **Speaker of the House**, and that placed him in a position of great influence in the House.

At the time, Inauguration Day was in March. That meant the House would have to act quickly. But they didn't meet right away. First, there had to be the usual back room bargaining and arm-twisting. Some representatives were putting the word out that their votes could be "bought" in exchange for cabinet posts. Perhaps a vote could even be gotten with the promise of an important ambassador assignment.

Clay was the best at making such deals. He had been collecting political debts for many years, and now it was time to call them in. His main goal was to set himself up for the next presidential election. He knew Andrew Jackson, having won both the popular vote and the Electoral College vote, would be his main opposition in the next presidential election. Therefore, his goal was to manipulate the vote in the House to make sure Jackson didn't get to be president this time.

In those days, the usual stepping stone to the presidency was the cabinet position of Secretary of State. Many suspected Clay might try to accomplish his goals by working a deal with Adams. The deal would be that if Clay could convince enough representatives to vote against Jackson, Adams would be elected president, and in exchange, Adams would select Clay as his Secretary of State. Clay believed that would put him in line for the presidency next time.

In actuality, Clay disliked Adams, but he thought he would have a better chance against Adams than Jackson in the next election.

As soon as the other representatives saw Clay meeting privately with Adams, they knew the deal was on.

Once the deal was made, it was Clay's job to get representatives to change their votes and go for Adams. It wasn't easy because few liked Adams. But with threats and promises, Clay was able to pull it off.

The House met to vote on February 9, 1825, and John Quincy Adams won the votes of 13 states, exactly the number needed to win the presidency.

Adams immediately named Clay as his Secretary of State.

Jackson and his supporters were furious. They called the deal Clay and Adams had made a "corrupt bargain." The term stuck, and in the end, undid all of Clay's attempts to set himself up for the presidency in the next election.

When the word of the House's vote and the "corrupt bargain" got out, the people who had voted for Jackson were outraged. They saw him as the rightful president-elect, and they could not be consoled by the politicians telling them that it had all been done according to the rule of law as specified by the Constitution's section on the Electoral College.

Jackson came right out and said the whole thing was a travesty. He and his supporters asked what kind of system it was where the person who won both the popular vote *and* the Electoral College vote did not get to be president. He said the rights of the people had been bartered away, and called for an immediate end to the Electoral College system of electing the president. He demanded to know why the nation's most important office should not be elected *directly by the people.*

Although just about everybody agreed that the corrupt deal method of selecting a president was not fair, the smaller-population states were completely united in their desire to keep the Electoral College system. In the first place, the two extra electoral votes each of the smaller states got gave them an advantage in determining who the president would be. And they didn't want to change the system of letting the House of Representatives decide close elections, because if the House decided the presidency, every state got one vote, no matter how large or small the state was. That disproportionate advantage pretty much guaranteed Jackson's demand for an end to the Electoral College system would be ignored by the smaller states. And because such a change would require an amendment to the Constitution and ratification by three-fourths of states, even Jackson knew changing it would never happen.

The dissatisfaction with the results of the election of 1824 led to a significant change in the American political landscape. Jackson declared that he would run again in 1828, and because of the unfairness of how the 1824 election had turned out, many predicted he would win this time.

The senator from New York, Martin Van Buren, saw the people's anger at the way Jackson had been denied the presidency through back-room dealings as an opportunity to enhance his own fortunes. In the 1824 election, he had been a supporter of Crawford, but when it became clear that the people wanted the "outsider" Jackson instead of the usual Washington insider, he switched his allegiance and declared it was time for a new Jacksonian democracy. He said it would be a democracy of the common man instead of a political monopoly by the eastern elites (although he himself might accurately have been described as being part of that cadre).

Van Buren and Jackson broke with the all-powerful Democratic-Republican party. (Modern day Democrats now see that moment as the starting point of the Democratic party, and they claim Andrew Jackson as the party's founder.)

Leading up to the 1828 presidential election, the so-called **Jacksonian movement** gradually grew in political strength. It was a coalition of farmers and low-wage Irish-Catholic laborers. It was strongest in the states with the largest populations, which in those days included Virginia, New York, and Pennsylvania. This new **"democratic"** party was "for the people" and quite vocally against the "rich and the powerful."

In line with that belief, they fought to get rid of **voting rules** that said only men of property, or men who paid taxes, were allowed to vote. They said all white men should be allowed to vote. (It took many more years to accomplish that goal. By 1850, *nearly* all the "property requirements" had been eliminated in the *majority* of the states.)

The Jacksonian Democrats also believed America had a **"manifest destiny"** to expand throughout the American West, possibly all the way to the Pacific coast. However, they were against the expansion of slavery into the West.

The Jacksonians were against unlimited expansion of centralized federal power, but they could not be called states' righters because they believed the power should be in the hands of the people, not in the hands of the rich and powerful who normally ran politics. They strongly believed the Electoral College took power away from the people and put it into the hands of those rich and powerful politicians. They were also against the idea that it was the rich and powerful who appointed the members of United States Senate, but again there were frustrated by **the smaller-population states who didn't want the people to elect senators**. The South especially was against direct election of either presidents or senators because they were afraid the large states of the North would vote for men who might try to end slavery.

On the other hand, the Jacksonian democrats did generally favor **a** *laissez-faire* approach to economics; that is, they believed the federal government should not try to regulate businesses.

They also believed in a "**hard money system**" in which only gold and silver could be considered true currency. They were suspicious of banks, and were against the idea of a government bank.

The Jacksonian Democrats were in favor of the "**spoils system.**" The basic concept of the spoils system was that **to the victor shall go the spoils**; that is, a newly elected government official had the right to fire all of the previous administration's political appointees and bring in their own people.

COMMENT:

The Jacksonian Democrats' innovation of the **spoils system** is still in place today. Whenever a new president is elected, he gets rid of a large percentage of the former administration's top-level employees and surrounds himself with the party loyalists who helped get him elected. The reasoning of the Jacksonian Democrats was that only through the adoption of the spoils system could an administration be held accountable for their failures. It is the "buck stops here" concept, meaning the president makes all the personnel appointments; therefore he should be responsible for their failures.

However, although modern day presidents still use the spoils system to replace many of the nation's top government officials as soon as they are elected, they now seem less willing to take the blame when things go wrong.

The Presidential Election of 1828

As a result of the national outrage over the fact that Andrew Jackson did not get to be president despite winning the vote in 1824 pretty much assured him the win in 1828. He and his running mate, John C. Calhoun from South Carolina, won easily. It would mark the beginning of an era of "**Jacksonian democracy**" that tried to take political power out of the hands of the rich and powerful "elitists."

COMMENT:

In response to Jackson's being elected president in 1828, Henry Clay and John Quincy Adams put together an oppositional coalition in Congress to fight against Jackson's new **Democratic Party**. Eventually, they took on the name "**Whigs**." (There was a Whig party in England that fought against the absolute rule of monarchy, and in America the term had been taken up as a reference to those who fought against tyranny.)

However, at first, the Whigs were not able to persuade the people that their plans for the nation were better than those of the Democrats. For one thing, they were against the popular idea of westward expansion, insisting that modernization of the still-undeveloped nation in the East was more important. They felt Jackson and the Democrats were holding the nation back from modernization.

The Whigs *did* find support among the professional classes, business owners, and the owners of large plantations, but there were not enough voters in those groups to carry the next presidential election. When Clay ran for president as a Whig against Jackson in 1832, he got only 49 electoral votes as compared to Jackson's 219.

However, the Whig's plans to modernize the cities and the nation's manufacturers struck a chord in the cities that depended on manufacturing for their existence. As a result, the Whigs did win the vote in some cites even though the Democratic campaigns characterizing the Whigs as elites cost them a lot of votes among the poor.

The Democrats continued to describe the Whigs as the party of the rich and powerful, and that message resonated with the Irish-Catholic immigrants that had tended to settle in the eastern cities.

Some Protestant ministers, favoring the Whigs, tried to discredit the Irish-Catholics, telling their congregations that Jackson and his followers were immoral, and that a vote for the Democrats was a vote for immorality. Protestant reformers railed against drinking and whoring, and they proposed a national prohibition on sales of alcohol that would put and end to what they saw as "the liquor problem" in America.

Within a generation, the Whig Party was able to put up a candidate in nearly every election, and they gradually began to have more success.

The Whigs main agenda was to create an "**American system**" of rapid industrial growth and government support for manufacturers. They proposed high tariffs against foreign imports that might compete with American manufactured products. They were also in favor of government support of banking, and they felt the government should get involved in the expansion of the nation's infrastructure of roads and canals and railroads, anything that would make America more of a manufacturing country instead of an agrarian country.

The Whigs also felt America's educational system was in great need of modernization. They wanted the national government to get involved in creating a better public school system.

It soon became apparent that the main difference between the two political parties was that the Whigs felt the national government should be stronger and more involved in developing the future of the nation as a whole, while the Democrats felt such things should be left to the states.

The Presidential Election of 1832

The presidential election of 1832 saw the Democratic incumbent, **Andrew Jackson**, win easily against **Henry Clay** of Kentucky. Jackson won 219 of the 286 electoral votes cast. ,However, a number of other candidates also received electoral votes, mostly from their own states. They included John Floyd (who was not officially a candidate) who won 11 electoral votes, Hugh L. White who won 47 electoral votes, and Daniel Webster who won 23 electoral votes.

Jackson was reelected in 1832, and soon the outrage over the Electoral College was forgotten as new political parties were developed and new ideologies sprang up. For the next decade, the national political argument would be focused on concerns about slavery and about how involved the national government should be in people's lives.

The Presidential Election of 1836

The Democrats **held onto the presidency in 1836** when Jackson supported his vice president **Martin Van Buren** for president. Kentucky Senator **Richard Mentor Johnson** was chosen as Van Buren's running mate.

The Whigs, knowing they would have little chance against Jackson's Democrats, focused on electing members of the House of Representatives in case of an electoral deadlock which would again send the choice of a president to the House (where each state would get one vote).

COMMENT:

The selection of Richard Mentor Johnson as the Democratic vice presidential candidate in 1836 was surprising to many because he was known to be having a sexual relationship with one of his female slaves. He was quite open about it. Although it was well known that some slave owners had sex with their slaves, it was not seen as appropriate to discuss it openly.

Johnson's first sexual relationship was with a slave named Julia Chinn. He described her as his common law wife and admitted that he was the father of her two daughters.

When Julia Chinn died in 1833, Johnson started a new relationship with another female slave, but she left him for another man. Johnson sent his men to capture her, sold her at auction, and took up with her sister.

In political circles, there was much talk about Johnson's history of sex with his slaves, and even more talk about his unwillingness to keep quiet about it. As a result, when Van Buren ran for reelection in 1840, the Democratic party refused to endorse Johnson as Van Buren's running mate. Nevertheless, Van Buren stuck with him.

Van Buren was defeated in his bid for reelection, and Johnson went back to Kentucky. In 1850, he was again elected to the to the Kentucky House of Representatives.

Johnson saw to it that both of Chinn's daughters were provided with an education and arranged for them both to marry white men. Nevertheless, when Johnson died, the local judge ruled that he left no legal children and divided Johnson's considerable holdings between his brothers.

The Presidential Election of 1840

The **economic panic of 1837** had hurt the U.S. economy during Van Buren term in office. The people blamed the poor economy on the restrictive economic policies of **the Jacksonian Democrats**. As is common today, when the economy turns bad, the people vote against whatever political party is in power. That was the main reason why Van Buren's run for reelection failed.

In 1840, the Whigs put up **William H. Harrison** from Ohio He chose **John Tyler**, a U.S. Senator from Virginia.

Harrison was seen as a military hero for his role in victories against the Indians in the Northwest Indian War, and by campaigning against the economic policies of the Democrats, Harrison was able to defeat the incumbent president, Van Buren to **become the first Whig president**. However, Harrison died from pneumonia after only 32 days in office, and **Vice President Tyler** served out the rest of his term.

Although Tyler had been elected as a Whig, he disagreed with many of their proposals, and while he was still serving as president, he was thrown out of the Whig Party.

The Presidential Election of 1844

In the election of 1844, the issue of slavery became a major point of contention. **The Whigs again put up Clay, a slave owner**. Most of the Democrats wanted to nominate Van Buren again, but his stance against the expansion of slavery to new states meant the Southern states would be unified against him.

After a contentious Democratic nominating convention, **James K. Polk**, a slave owner from Tennessee, emerged as the compromise candidate. He promised to serve only one term if elected and the Democrats decided to nominate him.

Polk won over Clay in a fairly close election, and was serving as president when statehood was granted to Texas, leading to **the Mexican-American War**.

COMMENT:

Unlike the War of 1812, the American people *were not* solidly behind **the Mexican-American War**. Democratic president Polk encouraged **the annexation of Texas** as part of his plan to expand the United States all the way to the Pacific Ocean even though it was almost sure to result in a war with Mexico. The Whig Party and anti-slavery groups were both against the annexation of Texas, and although their reasons for the opposition differed, it was one cause they were able to agree on.

In 1836, the Americans in the **Texas territory** had raised an army and had, after several bloody battles, defeated the troops of General Antonio López de Santa Anna, the dictator of Mexico. At the conclusion of that struggle, Texas declared itself to be an independent territory.

One of the main reasons the Texans had declared their independence from Mexico was that the Mexican government had tried to enforce its government policy forbidding the practice of slavery, and as soon as the declaration of Texan independence was official, many of the larger landholders began bringing in slaves from the American South to use in their farming and ranching enterprises. By 1845, slavery was a well-established practice in Texas, and that was the reason American anti-slavery groups were against granting Texas statehood.

Of course, the Southern states were strongly in favor of granting Texas statehood, because it was a slave state. At that time, most of the territories petitioning for statehood were in the North and the Southern states feared there would soon be enough non-slave states to outvote them in Congress. They knew that could mean the end of slavery in the United States.

Despite the anti-slavery protests and the opposition of the Whigs, in 1845, Texas' petition to become a state was granted.

At that time, Mexico was having its own internal battles, but they were united in their position that Texas still belonged to Mexico. As soon as Texas was granted statehood, Mexico said it would lead to war.

President Polk sent representatives to Mexico City to try to forestall hostilities, even offering Mexico huge amounts of money as compensation, but Mexico would not negotiate. They felt reclaiming what they saw as the theft of a piece of their country was a matter of national honor.

After the failure of negotiations, President Polk sent troops to establish a fort on the banks of the Rio Grande river. In response, Mexico sent 2,000 cavalry troops to the area. Accidentally, they ran into a small U.S. Army patrol and they killed 16 U.S. soldiers.

In response, President Polk declared, "Mexico has passed the boundary of the United States, has invaded our territory and shed American blood upon American soil." He demanded Congress grant a declaration of war against Mexico. After a short, but bitter, debate, they did so with the unanimous support of the Southern Democrats.

Americans were divided over the war. Many in the North felt it was a war designed to spread slavery to the West.

Others, knowing that Mexico also controlled California, thought it might be a chance to grab California as well. There was also much talk about "manifest destiny" and the United States being from "sea to shining sea."

The Whigs, including Abraham Lincoln, continued to lobby against the war, the preparations for the coming battle went on unabated. Polk sent troops under the command of General Zachary Taylor into Mexico, and ordered naval forces to the Mexican coast in support.

At the same time, U.S. forces invaded California, and within a year, they controlled California from San Diego to San Francisco. On January 13, 1847, the **Treaty of Cahuenga** signifying the surrender of California was signed by the opposing military forces near what is now Los Angeles.

General Taylor went deeper into Mexico and General Santa Ana brought troops north from Mexico City to meet him. After extended fighting, Santa Ana was forced to retreat.

President Polk also sent a second army under General Winfield Scott to invade Mexico by sea. Santa Ana's army rallied to meet that advance, but was again routed.

Scott pushed on deeper into Mexico and soon captured Mexico City. Faced with the possible loss of even more territory, Mexico had no choice but to surrender. On February 2, 1848, Mexico signed **the Treaty of Guadalupe Hidalgo**, agreeing to the Texas boundaries specified by the United States.

Despite the relatively easy victory over Mexico, the people of the United States were still divided over the war and over the issue of slavery being expanded into the new Western territories. It is worth noting here that President Ulysses S. Grant, who fought in Mexico under General Taylor, said in his later memoirs that the Civil War was largely the outgrowth of the Mexican-American war.

The Presidential Election of 1848

During the election of 1848, slavery was becoming an even more contentious issue than it had been in previous elections.

Zachary Taylor, a Virginia slave owner ran as a Whig and defeated **Lewis Cass** of Michigan in another close election, with each candidate carrying 15 states. If Cass had been able to carry New York, the Electoral College vote would have ended in a tie and the decision about who was president would have again been sent to the House of Representatives.

The Presidential Election of 1852

In **the election of 1852,** the Democratic presidential nominating convention at first got nowhere because of constant arguing about how to deal with the issue of slavery. When they finally did get around to the nominations, there were four strong candidates and therefore the voting got nowhere. Finally, **Franklin Pierce**, who was not one of the four main candidates, was put up as a compromise candidate and eventually was selected. Pierce was from the small state of New Hampshire, a non-slave state. However, he was known to favor allowing slavery to be practiced in the new western states. His main attribute as far as the Democrats were concerned was that he had fought in the Mexican-American War and had been so valued as a leader of men that he had risen to the rank of brigadier general of volunteers.

The Whigs nominating convention also had to deal with agitation over the slavery issue, but in the end, the party leaders decided to support the **Compromise of 1850,** which was a compromise that forced Texas to surrendered its claim to New Mexico, and allowed

California to come in as a free state. However, the South added language to the compromise that allowed new states to decide for themselves whether to allow slavery or not. That overturned the prior **Missouri Compromise** of 1821 which made slavery illegal north of the **Compromise Line** (any territory north of latitude 36° 30' North which marked the northern border of Missouri). The South was also able to insert the **Fugitive Slave Act** into the compromise which made it illegal for slaves to run away to the north and specified that if they did, the North had to return them to their rightful owners.

After much contention, the Whigs finally nominated **Winfield Scott**, another Virginian from a slave-holding family who had made his name as a general in the Mexican-American war. Although his family still owned many slaves, he made it known that he was against expanding slavery to the West.

The issue of slavery was to play a big part in the presidential election of 1852. People were note sure of the Whig position on slavery. Scott was a slave owner, but he said he was against expanding slavery into the new Western states. Because Scott's stated position on slavery was not in line with the wishes of the Southern states, he did not get the solid support from Southern voters he expected, and as a result, Pierce, a relative unknown, won the election.

COMMENT:

Most people thought **General Winfield Scott** would be elected president simply because he was **a military hero** in the Mexican-American War and in the Indian Wars.

However, the Mexican-American War was not fully supported by most Americans because of the slavery issue in Texas. And there were rumors that his **"victories" over the Indians** included almost-unbelievable **cruelty to non-combatant Native Americans**.

Although most Americans supported the idea of moving the Indians off their land and onto reservations, the citizens of the East did not support excessive cruelty while doing it. News about the terrible treatment of the Indians leaked out, diminishing Scott's reputation as a military hero.

However, in Scott's defense, it should be pointed out that he was just carrying out policies that had been around for a long time. A policy of "civilizing" American Indians had been in place since the presidency of George Washington. Under Washington, Indian agents were assigned to make the Indians give up their nomadic hunting and gathering ways and force them to settle down to farming.

They Indian tribes were also encouraged to break up the communal lands and assign property ownership the individual Indian families. The problem was, as soon as that was done, the land could be sold, and through various means, some legal and some not so legal means, much of what had been Indian lands ended up in the hands of white settlers.

Many Indian tribes, including the Cherokee, Chickasaw, Choctaw, Creek, and Seminole, resisted resettlement, so Congress passed the **Indian Removal Act**. President Jackson signed it into law at the beginning of the summer of 1830. It was deemed that the tribes would resettle to unclaimed land far to the west, into what is now Oklahoma, an area that was henceforth deemed to be "Indian lands."

By law, communal Indian lands were considered sovereign. That meant they were not under the control of the United States, and therefore could only be acquired by the United States through treaties. However, pursuant to the Indian Removal Act, the Indians were put into a position of either signing treaties that would give them *some* payment for their lands and the right to settle in new land in the West, or face the prospect of being forcibly removed and getting nothing. Many signed, but many others refused to leave their ancestral lands. Some used the services of sympathetic lawyers to try to fight the act, but had little success. A key 1823 Supreme Court decision stated that Indians could only *occupy* land within the United States; they could not legally hold title to those lands.

In 1838, General Scott was sent to forcibly move the Indians off their lands and into holding camps. General Scott wanted to use regular troops to do the job, hoping they would treat the Indians more humanely than the locals, but none were available, so he had to use the local militia. Almost all of the 7,000 militiamen that participated were local citizens who were glad to get rid of the Indians so they could take over their lands.

By the time it was over, the newspapers were proudly reporting that Scott's troops had captured or killed every Indian in Alabama, Georgia, North Carolina, and Tennessee. Those that were captured were sent to concentration camps near the U.S. Indian Agency near Cleveland, Tennessee. Then, they were sent West.

In the dead of winter of 1838, most of the remaining Native Americans, including almost all of the 15,000 Indians that were part of the Cherokee nation, were forced to walk one thousand miles west to the new reservations. Most had little warm clothing and some were barefoot. Many had contracted smallpox while being held in the concentration camps, and as a result, untold thousands died on the trail. It became known as the **Trail of Tears**.

The Presidential Election of 1856

By the time the election of 1856 came around, the Whig Party had been torn apart by the issue of slavery.

A new party, **the Republican Party**, emerged specifically to fight the spread of slavery to new states entering the Union.

The **Kansas Nebraska Act** of 1854 had created the new territories of Kansas and Nebraska, but the South had again used its unfair voting advantage in Congress to force language to be inserted into the law to allow the new states to determine for themselves whether or not to allow slavery. Once again, they ignored the previous compromise, known as **the Missouri Compromise,** which made slavery illegal north of Missouri.

President Pierce's handling of the contention over slavery in Kansas proved to be his undoing. His party, sensing defeat at the polls, refused to grant his request to be nominated for a second term. Instead, they nominated **John C. Fremont**, another Mexican-American war hero from the new state of California.

COMMENT:

The result of the **Kansas Nebraska Act** was immediate contention over the issue of slavery in the new states, especially in Kansas. Slave holders in Missouri flooded across the border into Kansas and created a territorial legislature in a town near the Missouri border. One of their first acts was to pass a law making Kansas a slave state.

In response, a "**free soil**" group set up an opposing legislature in Topeka. They declared the slave holder's legislation invalid. The "free soil" advocates opposed what they called "**slave power**." Slave power was the idea that the Southern slave states had so much inordinate power in Congress and in electing the president, they would be able to move into any new state and establish it as a slave state. Then they would buy up all the land, and bring in slaves.

Tensions escalated when an armed group of pro-slavery men attacked the free-state town of Lawrence Kansas to destroy the anti-slavery newspaper offices. They burned buildings and stole everything they could get their hands on from the homes of the citizens.

Senator Charles Sumner of Massachusetts denounced the attacks in Kansas, and in response, Preston Smith Brooks, a congressman from South Carolina came into the Senate chambers and attacked Sumner with a cane. The senators who were present tried to stop the attack, but some of the Southern representatives pulled out pistols and held them back to let the attack go on. Sumner was beaten so badly he was bedridden for years and was unable to return to the Senate.

Soon, John Brown, a well-known anti-slavery advocate, went to Kansas and entered the fray. One of his first acts was to lead an attack on a pro-slavery settlement at Pottawatomie Creek where he and his supporters killed five men.

As the tensions escalated, Congress passed a resolution declaring the pro-slavery legislature illegal in Kansas and the resolutions they had passed as improperly done.

But President Pierce ignored the congressional resolution and continued to recognize the pro-slavery legislature. Then he outraged the North by sending federal troops to break up the anti-slavery legislature.

Emboldened by the support of the president, Missouri pro-slavery men formed an army and marched into Kansas.

In what was to become known as the time of **Bleeding Kansas**, battles between the pro-slavery forces and the anti-slavery forces continued for years, foreshadowing the terrible Civil War that was to come.

When the American Civil War did finally break out a few years later, Kansas continued to be a battleground between North and South.

In opposition to **John C. Fremont**, the Whig's candidate in the 1856 election, the Democrats nominated Senator **James Buchanan** from Pennsylvania. Buchanan won the election, however, the relatively unknown Fremont had managed to carry 33% of the popular vote, which is remarkable given that he got **no votes at all in the South**. This established the Republican Party as a viable political force in the United States.

Chapter Seven

The Election of Lincoln and a Country in Crisis

The Presidential Election of 1860

The presidential election of 1860 was the most contentious election in the history of the nation, and it led directly to the Civil War. The contention about slavery that had divided the nation for so long, was about to break out in armed conflict.

Throughout the history of the United States, **the South had tried to maintain enough of a voting advantage in Congress** to block new free states from joining the Union. Most other nations had already outlawed slavery, so the South knew that if they allowed a majority of even one free state to exist in Congress, the voting power of the North would make it likely that sooner or later Congress would vote to outlaw slavery.

The South's control of Congress and the Electoral College went all the way back to the founding of the nation when they had refused to join the Union unless they got extra power in both Congress and the election of presidents. Eight of the original thirteen states, Delaware, New Jersey, Georgia, New York, Maryland, South Carolina, Virginia, and North Carolina allowed slavery, and they always voted as a block.

However, as the nation grew in the mid-1800s, more free states joined the Union. Up until then, the South had managed to use their veto power in Congress to maintain the balance between slave states and free states. By 1848, there were fifteen slave states, Delaware, Georgia, Maryland, South Carolina, Virginia, North Carolina, Kentucky, Tennessee, Louisiana, Mississippi, Alabama, Missouri, Arkansas, Florida, and Texas. There were fifteen free states, New Jersey, Pennsylvania, Connecticut, Massachusetts, New Hampshire, New York, Rhode Island, Vermont, Ohio, Indiana, Illinois, Maine, Michigan, Iowa, and Wisconsin. But as a result of the Mexican-

American War, in 1850, California was brought in as a free state and that upset the balance.

Soon, other western states petitioned to join the Union. As we have seen, the Kansas Nebraska Act of 1854 made it possible that these new states could become slave states, and the Republican Party was formed to fight against that possibility.

In 1856, to make their point, the Republicans had nominated **John C. Fremont** for president simply because he was from the new free state of California.

When two more western states, **Minnesota and Oregon, joined the Union** in 1858 and 1859, they also chose not to become slave states.

For the South, the handwriting was on the wall. They had lost their voting advantage in both the Senate and in the Electoral College, and it was clear that sooner or later, the Northern states would elect a president that would lead to an effort to abolish slavery.

That was the situation leading into the presidential election of 1860. It was clear that slavery would be the main issue in the election, and the issue was sending the American political situation into chaos. New political movements were springing up as special-interest groups fought to gain control over both local and national political interests.

The Democrats held their 1860 presidential nominating convention in Charleston, South Carolina, which assured that there would be plenty of agitation from the local pro-slavery groups.

Senator Stephen A. Douglas was from the free state of Illinois, but he had been a key proponent of the Kansas Nebraska Act which allowed states to decide for themselves whether to allow slavery or not, so many in the party thought he would make a good compromise candidate. He had made a name for himself as a capable orator in his campaign against **Abraham Lincoln** for an Illinois Senate seat.

But the Democratic Party was deeply divided. The **Supreme Court's Dred Scott decision** of 1857 had shocked the nation by declaring that the Constitution protected slavery in the United States, and the party leaders knew that the nation's voters would be paying as much attention to the party's stance on slavery as to what candidate they nominated.

Many Southern hard liners insisted the Democratic party should openly take a pro-slavery stance and try to elect a president that would fight for legislation to make slavery legal in all states. But now that the South had lost their advantage in the Electoral College, the party leaders knew that would all but guarantee a loss in the upcoming election.

By the time balloting began, six major candidates had been put forward for the Democratic nomination. In the first ballot, Douglas led, but by not enough to be the nominee. There were just too many staunch pro-slavery delegates against him. The balloting went on and on with much pro-slavery agitation until finally, after 57 ballots, the delegates voted to adjourn the convention and meet again later in a Northern city.

By the time the Democrats met again two months later in Baltimore, there was contention as to whether the troublesome pro-slavery delegates from the South should even be admitted. In the heated debate that resulted, all of the Southern delegates walked out, thus assuring Douglas's nomination. As a compromise, Senator Benjamin Fitzpatrick of Alabama was nominated for vice president, but he refused to run with Douglas and was replaced by former Senator Herschel V. Johnson of Georgia.

The Southern delegates who had walked out held their own convention and nominated John C. Breckinridge from Kentucky for president and Joseph Lane from North Carolina for vice president.

COMMENT:

The Supreme Court's Dred Scott decision of 1857 caused an uproar throughout the North. The court had been asked to decide if Dred Scott, a slave who been taken by his master to the free state of Illinois was free or still a slave. He had been legally married while in Illinois, even though slaves were not supposed to have any legal rights, including the right to marry. The court, in a seven to two decision, shocked the Northern free states by stating that slaves were not legal citizens of the United States and therefore had no legal right to appeal to the court. The majority members of the Supreme Court went on to state that slaves were private property even if they were taken to a free state. They said a slave could not be taken away from his or her owner without due process.

> Unexpectedly, the court's decision triggered the economic panic of 1857 when investors, anticipating trouble, suddenly lost faith in their investments.

The 1860 Republican presidential nominating convention was held in Chicago a month after the debacle of the Democrat's convention in South Carolina.

The favorite candidate going into the Republican convention was former New York Governor William H. Seward, and he led after the first two ballots. But when he failed to rally any more delegates to his side, a local Illinois dark horse, Abraham Lincoln, was nominated. He had gained some national notoriety as a calm and effective orator in his series of debates with Stephen Douglas during their race for an Illinois Senate seat.

Of special note was the Republican Party's written platform: it stated that slavery would not be allowed to spread any further.

The 1860 presidential election ballots included the following candidates: **Abraham Lincoln**, Republican; **Stephen Douglas**, Democrat; **John Breckenridge**, Southern Democrat; **John Bell**, Constitutional Union.

The result was that the Southern votes were split between Breckenridge, Bell, and Douglas, leading to a relatively easy victory for Lincoln.

Immediately after Lincoln's election, seven Southern states, South Carolina, Mississippi, Florida, Alabama, Georgia, Louisiana, and Texas **seceded from the Union**. When hostilities commenced with the Confederate forces attacking Fort Sumter in South Carolina on April 12, 1861, four additional states, Virginia, Arkansas, North Carolina, and Tennessee joined the Confederacy.

COMMENT:

The causes and effects of the **American Civil War** are beyond the scope of a book about the Electoral College and how U.S. presidents are elected. Thousands of other books have discussed the Civil War, and its causes and consequences have been covered in great detail.

But I should point out that it was the biased Electoral College system, along with the two votes each Southern state got in the U.S. Senate, plus the extra votes the South got in the House of Representatives by the counting of millions of slaves as part of their population, that kept the South in the Union as long as it did. The South's extra voting power in the Electoral College resulted in ten of the first twelve presidents being Southern slave holders, and they made sure slavery continued to be the law of the land.

Even after Northerners began to be elected president, the South was able to use their voting power to keep a balance between slave states and free states. That ended up making the United States the last major country in the world to abolish slavery.

As soon as the Civil War started, President Lincoln took a hands-on approach. He personally supervised the North's war strategy and selected the generals to fight it. And when he was disappointed with the performances of his generals, he replaced them.

Eventually, Lincoln selected General **Ulysses S. Grant,** a military leader who was having great success in the West. Lincoln called him to Washington and named him to be his top general.

Lincoln knew he was going to have to try to hold the nation together throughout a war that would pit friends and family against each other, but he also wanted to live up to his promise to end slavery. During his first term in office, he announced the Emancipation Proclamation, and urged Congress to pass an amendment to the Constitution outlawing slavery.

He appointed five judges to the Supreme Court, all of them well known for their anti-slavery positions. But he did not want the nation to be forever divided, so long before the war ended, he was already proposing plans for the reconstruction of the South.

The Presidential Election of 1864

Despite the terrible loss of human life in the war, Lincoln was again nominated by the Republicans for reelection in 1864.

However, Lincoln was unhappy with his vice president, Hannibal Hamlin. He replaced him with Andrew Johnson. It was a decision that was to have a profound effect on Johnson's life.

The Democrats put up General **George B. McClellan**, the general Lincoln had demoted early in the war.

McClellen won only a few states. Lincoln won reelection, and because there was no Southern vote, it was an easy victory.

In the days after Lincoln's reelection, the war dragged on into yet another spring. However, Lincoln was sure the war would soon be over. The Confederate Army was exhausted and in retreat, but the Southern leadership was still not ready to give in.

The Union Army marched deeper into the Southern states, freeing millions of slaves as they went. At Lincoln's request, some of the slaves were recruited into black regiments of the Union Army.

Extended Union Army forays into the South, such as Sherman's infamous **March to the Sea,** destroyed much of the South's ability to continue the war.

Lee understood that continuing to fight would only result in more pointless bloodshed He finally surrendered his army to General Grant at Appomattox, Virginia on April 9, 1865.

A week later, even as the nation continued to celebrate the end of long and terrible war, Lincoln was assassinated by **John Wilkes Booth**, a well-known actor who was secretly a spy being supported by the Confederate secret service

Lincoln's vice president, **Andrew Johnson**, was sworn in as president the next morning, and for the next four years, he oversaw the rebuilding of the nation. He was known as a compromiser who repeatedly vetoed Congressional bills that were designed to punish the South or to give more rights to the freed slaves.

When Congress passed the bill to create the Fourteenth Amendment, he vetoed it. The amendment provided civil rights to all U.S. citizens, including freed slaves, and included an Equal Protection Clause that *required* each state to provide equal protection under the law to *all* people within its jurisdiction.

Congress quickly overrode Johnson's veto, and there was a move to impeach him. The vote in the House of Representatives to remove Johnson from office failed by only one vote.

Chapter Eight
Democrats Versus Republicans

The Presidential Election of 1868

Shunned by the Republican Party, for the election of 1868, Johnson sought reelection support from the Democrats. But they didn't want him either. Instead, they nominated Horatio Seymour, the former governor of New York.

The Republicans quickly nominated war hero, General Ulysses S. Grant who won both the general election and the Electoral College vote.

However, Seymour, the Democratic nominee, shocked the nation by winning his home state of New York, and it was said if Southern voters would have been allowed to vote in 1868, the outcome of the election would have been quite different. An accusation of voter fraud in New York was put forth and a Congressional investigation was initiated, but in the end, no action was taken.

The Presidential Election of 1872

In the presidential election of 1872, Grant easily won reelection, but five other candidates also won Electoral College votes. New York newspaper owner, Horace Greeley, came in second in the popular vote, but died before the Electoral College met. (Despite his not being alive, three electors voted for him anyhow).

The electoral votes from five southern state were questioned, and the electoral votes of Arkansas and Louisiana were rejected due to clear evidence of voter fraud and intimidation of African-American voters.

The Presidential Election of 1876

The election of 1876 was one of the most controversial in the history of the United States.

For president, the Republicans nominated **Rutherford B. Hayes**, the former governor of Ohio. He chose as his vice president, **William Wheeler**, a U.S. Representative from New York.

Hayes was a compromise candidate, selected after many ballots at the Republican nominating convention failed to produce a clear winner.

The Democrats nominated Governor **Samuel J. Tilden** of New York. Tilden had gained national recognition for managing to finally send New York's corrupt Boss Tweed to prison

---

COMMENT:

Politics during the eighteenth century was a rough and tumble business. Although some may say politics in our current era is mostly run by the rich, it was clearly so in New York in the mid 1800s.

William Tweed, known as "**Boss Tweed**," was one of the largest landowners in the state of New York, and he was a director of railroads and banks. He was elected to Congress in 1852, and later served in the New York state Senate.

After that, he got himself appointed to various city positions in which he could dispense political favors -- for a price. By controlling New York City boards and commissions, he was able to gain great influence over local politics, and even more influence over how public money was spent. Over time, he was able to create a political machine that controlled much of New York's politics. He became known as the "Grand Sachem" of Tammany Hall.

The end of his "reign" came when Governor Tilden worked with local prosecutors to convict him of stealing millions of dollars of public money through various schemes. The prosecution said he paid "workers" huge payments for mostly nonexistent city building projects just to get kickbacks. They gave examples such as the plasterer who had been paid over a hundred thousand dollars for a day's work and a carpenter who had been paid over three hundred thousand dollars for doing woodwork carpentry in a building that turned out not to have any woodwork in it (this in era during which the average urban New England worker made about $300 **per year**).

Tweed was imprisoned, and a million dollar bail was set. He had no trouble raising that much money and was therefore released.

Unbelievably, while all this was going on, Tweed was re-elected to the state senate.

But soon, he was arrested again, and this time the bail was raised to eight million dollars, an astounding amount of money in that era. Again, he had no trouble raising it.

But it was clear his empire was falling apart. His associates were also being arrested, and some of them were being convicted despite Tweed's attempts to subvert the legal process.

Tweed was finally convicted of corruption and graft and given a prison sentence of twelve years. But when the local jailers allowed him out for a "home visit," he escaped and fled to Spain. He was eventually caught there and put on an American warship to be brought back to the United States.

Now apparently out of money and desperate to get out of prison, he said he would tell prosecutors all about how his corruption system worked if they would release him. An agreement was reached that resulted in the prosecution of many members of his inner ring.

After confessing, Tweed was ready to get out of prison so he could to try to reestablish his empire. But Governor Tilden refused to let him go. Tweed was held in a local New York City jail until his death in 1878.

Everyone knew the election of 1876 was going to be close. The Democrats were resurgent, especially in the South, and with the retirement of General Grant, they felt they had a good chance to take the presidency back from the Republicans. The Democrats tried to paint the Republicans as involved in graft and political manipulation, and contrasted them with Tilden who had a reputation as a reformer.

The Republicans main approach to the campaign was to remind the people that it was the Democrats that had caused the Civil War through their support of slavery.

The Democrats referred to this tactic as "waving the bloody shirt," and pointed out that not every Democrat had been a rebel. They reminded the voters that both Tilden and his running mate, **Thomas Hendricks**, were Northerners. They called for **an end to reconstruction** and a return to normalcy. It was a message that appealed to a war-exhausted country.

During the election, Southern paramilitary groups such as the **Red Shirts** and the **White League** disrupted Republican rallies and used violence and intimidation to try to stop Republicans, and especially blacks, from voting.

When the results of the popular vote were in, Tilden, the choice of the Southern states, had apparently won by 252,666 votes, the closest national vote in history.

However, there were cries of fraud with regard to the counting of votes in the South. The Republicans claimed their voters in Florida had either not been allowed to vote or had been tricked into voting for the wrong candidate by deceptively designed ballots. They cited numerous instances of voter intimidation and fraud in Florida, pointing out that documents certifying the election there had been signed by the state attorney-general, a Democratic, and by the Florida governor, also a Democrat (as we shall see in a later chapter, Al Gore's supporters were later to make similar accusations regarding the 2000 election in Florida).

Reports of voter intimidation and ballot fraud were also raised in Louisiana, and South Carolina. One of the Democratic tricks in the South was to print a picture of Abraham Lincoln on the Democratic ballot to try to get illiterate voters to select that one.

In addition, because the Constitution did not stipulate that Electoral College electors *had to* vote for the popular vote winner, there was no assurance that Southern Democratic electors would be willing to cast their votes for the anti-slavery Republicans.

When the ballots of the Electoral College voters were counted, it appeared that Hayes had won by one vote. But neither candidate had the requisite 185 electoral votes that were required for a majority. It appeared that once again the selection of the president would be done in the House of Representatives (at that time, the House was controlled by the Republicans).

Because of the many accusations of voter fraud in the South, Congress created a special commission to review the results. All that did was lead to more contention about who should be appointed to the special commission. In the end, the Democrats (who controlled the Senate because of the two senators given to each Southern state) were allowed to appoint five members, and the Republicans (who controlled the population-based House of Representatives) were also allowed to appoint five. Four Supreme Court justices were added to the commission, two with Republican leanings, and two with Democratic leanings. Those four Supreme Court justices were allowed to select one more justice to serve on the committee, and they chose Justice David Davis who they saw as politically independent. Hoping to gain a deciding vote on the committee, the Democratically-controlled Illinois senate immediately appointed Davis to fill their vacant U.S. Senate seat. But their plan backfired when Davis resigned from the Supreme Court to become a senator. The four justices selected Justice Joseph P. Bradley who was supposed to be another impartial member of the court.

In January of 1877, the special Congressional committee met to examine the results of the Electoral College votes from Florida, Louisiana, Oregon, and South Carolina. If the committee hoped for easy answers, they were disappointed: those states each presented two conflicting sets of Electoral College results, one from the Republicans and one from the Democrats.

After much debate, the Congressional members of the committee voted right along party lines. That meant the vote was a tie. The decision was up to Justice Bradley. He voted with the Republicans, making the decision 8-7 in favor of giving the disputed Electoral College votes to Hayes. That gave Hayes a 185-184 Electoral College victory.

The election of 1876 is the only election in the history of the United States in which a candidate **received an absolute majority of the popular vote and did not get to be president** (although Al Gore won the popular vote in the 2000 election by 543,895 votes, because a third-party candidate also received votes, Gore did not win an absolute majority).

It is not clear under what authority Congress made their decision because there is no indication in the Electoral College section of the Constitution that there is any way the winner of the Electoral College vote can be denied the presidency.

Most people in the South thought the election had been stolen from Tilden by the North, but the people of the North felt it was the right decision because at that time there were very large populations of former slaves in the South, and most people felt that if they had they been allowed to vote, they would have easily carried the election for Hayes.

The Presidential Election of 1880

In the 1880 presidential election, the popular vote was extremely close with **James Garfield**, a Republican from Ohio, getting 4,453,337 votes to Democrat **Winfield Scott Hancock**'s 4,444,267 votes. With a tiny national margin of only 9,070 votes, you would expect the Electoral College to end in a tie. But because of the strange winner-take-all system which had by then been accepted by almost every state, Garfield won by 214 to 155. To understand how that could happen, we have to look at the state-by-state results.

Of course, Garfield, the Republican, won all the Northern states, and Hancock, the Democrat, won all the Southern states. However, now that there were more Northern states in the Union, they had enough Electoral College votes to give Garfield the victory.

Interestingly, if only a few thousand voters in a handful of Northern states had voted for Hancock, he would have won both the popular vote and the Electoral College vote.

The Presidential Election of 1884

In the presidential election of 1884, a Democrat won for the first time in 28 years. Democrat **Grover Cleveland** beat Republican **James G. Blaine**, from Maine in a very close race. Cleveland won the national popular vote by a very narrow 57,579 margin, and by 219 to 182 in the Electoral College. He did it by winning the Southern states, and by winning Indiana, New Jersey, and most importantly New York. He won the popular vote in New York by only 1,149 votes, thereby gaining **all** of New York's 36 electoral votes. Had those 1,149 votes gone the other way, Cleveland would have still won the national popular vote, but Blaine would have been elected the nation's 20th president in the Electoral College.

The Presidential Election of 1888

In the presidential election of 1888, Democrat **Grover Cleveland** ran for reelection and won the popular vote. However, Republican **Benjamin Harrison** from Indiana got more Electoral College votes and was therefore elected president.

In the nationwide popular vote, Harrison got 5,443,633 to Cleveland's 5,538,163. Cleveland had won by 94,530 votes. So why wasn't he elected president? Once again, it was the strange workings of the Electoral College that determined who would be president, not the will of the people.

The reason Harrison won the Electoral College vote was because he was able to squeak out narrow popular vote margins in states with a lot of Electoral College votes. He won Illinois' 22 electoral votes and Michigan's 13 electoral votes and Missouri's 16 electoral votes by winning the popular vote by slim margins.

New York's 36 electoral votes were the main determining factor. Harrison won New York's 36 Electoral College votes by getting 14,373 more popular votes than Cleveland (out of 1,319,748 votes cast). For the second presidential election in a row, a few voters in one state determined by a narrow margin, who would get to be president, and this time it *was not* the candidate who won the popular vote.

Unlike the election of 1824, there was little public outrage in the North over the fact that the candidate chosen by the people did not get to be president because it was common knowledge that hundreds of thousands of former slaves were being kept away from the polls in the south. It was reasoned that those voters would have voted for Harrison if they had been given the opportunity.

Although there was little public outrage over the election of 1825, the result made it quite clear that close elections would continue to reveal the flaws of the Electoral College system.

The Presidential Election of 1892

The presidential election of 1892 demonstrated the same thing the election of 1824 had demonstrated: voters don't like it when the candidate they chose does not get to be president. They voted against the incumbent Benjamin Harrison and returned Grover Cleveland to the presidency.

Although the South was still solidly in the Democratic camp, six new Northern states, Idaho, North Dakota, South Dakota, Montana, Washington, and Wyoming voted for the first time in a presidential election, and they mostly supported the Republicans. (In this 1892 election, Wyoming became the only state to allow women to vote.)

COMMENT:

Although Wyoming women were allowed to vote in the presidential election of 1892, **Women's suffrage** in the United States did not come easily.

There was no serious movement in the United States to allow women to vote until 1848 when Gerrit Smith, a candidate for president, made it part of his Liberty Party's platform. However, at that time, the idea didn't get much traction.

By the mid 1850s, there was still no concerted effort on the part of the all-male political establishment to allow women to vote. However, women were starting to get some legal rights. In some states, a woman could file for divorce, and a few states passed laws that said working women didn't have to turn over their wages to their husbands.

Some states, especially Southern and rural states, were unwilling to give women *any* legal rights. A famous legal case in North Carolina made the point. A woman had appealed to change the state law so a woman would be allowed to file for divorce if she had been badly beaten by her husband. The state Supreme Court turned down her appeal in 1862, stating, "The law gives the husband power to use such a degree of force necessary to make the wife behave and know her place."

After the Civil War, there was some talk of Women's suffrage, but it took female activists like **Susan B. Anthony** to bring the issue to the public's attention. She and others like **Elizabeth Cady Stanton** organized women's rights gatherings and wrote books about the lack of women's legal rights in the U.S. Their books were intended to be read by women, but were also read by men. Some men voiced approval, but others tried to ban the books, saying for a women to have rights would be against the will of nature.

There was considerable resistance even among women's groups. Many women felt the suffragettes shouldn't be trying to change traditional women's roles.

Movements were formed to fight against the very idea of women gaining *any* legal rights, let alone the right to vote. One prominent organization was the **National Organization Against Women's Suffrage,** and it counted many women as members.

In 1869, Susan B. Anthony and Elizabeth Cady Stanton formed the **National Woman Suffrage Association (NWSA).** They lobbied for women's rights and proposed an amendment to the Constitution giving women the right to vote in all elections.

In 1890, several women's rights organizations came together to form the **National American Woman Suffrage Association** which was headed by **Carrie Chapman Catt**.

After Wyoming gave women the right to vote, lobbying efforts by Susan B. Anthony and others encouraged some of the other Western states to follow suit, apparently in hopes of attracting more women to the still untamed and almost all male Western territories.

Utah territory was one of the first Western states to allow women the vote, but it was not activist women who were behind the effort; it was activist men who were trying to stamp out the practice of polygamy. A group of men known as **Godbeites** left the Latter Day Saints (Mormon) church and took up the fight against the church-condoned practice of men having multiple wives. They hoped women, if given the right to vote, would be freed from the male dominance officially sanctioned by the Mormon Church and would vote to end polygamy.

The practice of men having multiple wives was part of the Mormon religion, but the church's leader, Brigham Young, got behind the women's suffrage movement effort in hopes it would help change the image of Utah women as oppressed, and maybe even sidetrack anti-polygamy legislation that was working its way through Congress. With Brigham Young's support, there was no resistance to the idea, and in 1869, the territorial legislature passed an act giving women the vote (but not the right to run for office).

Paradoxically, the U.S. Congress overrode the new Utah act by passing the **Edmunds-Tucker Anti-polygamy Act**, which specifically banned voting by women in Utah. The movement to stamp out polygamy in Utah was gaining momentum across the nation, and it was becoming a major issue in every presidential election. There was even a call to send U.S. Army troops to Utah to put a stop to the practice.

In 1890, the Mormon Church leaders declared that the church would no longer sanction the practice of polygamy. With that controversy out of the way, Utah was granted statehood in 1896 and **the right of Utah women to vote was written into the new state's constitution.**

In1865, Republicans proposed the **Fourteenth Amendment** to the Constitution that would give the vote to the millions of newly-freed black **men.**

It was not until 1915, long after the Emancipation Proclamation had given all **men** the right to vote, that Congress passed the **Nineteenth Amendment** to the Constitution which prohibited the states from denying the right to vote based on sex. Even at that late date, with the country becoming more and more industrialized and all of the lower 48 states now part of the Union, only some Western states and a few Midwestern states had granted women the right to vote. **Until 1915, women were specifically barred from voting** even in local elections in all of the East Coast states and most of the Southern states.

The Presidential Election of 1896

The presidential election of 1896 was contended mostly over economic matters. One contentious issue was about whether the U.S. should remain on **the gold standard**.

The Republicans nominated **William McKinley** who had served in the U.S. House of Representatives from Ohio, and as that state's governor.

The Democratic party was split over the issue of whether the U.S. should stay on the gold standard or not. After much contention, they nominated **William Jennings Bryan** who was against the gold standard and in favor of liberalizing the banking standards of the United States. Bryan was the youngest presidential nominee in American history, only one year older than the constitutional minimum of 35.

The election of 1896 was also one of the first elections in which campaign money played an important role. **The Republican campaign outspent the Democratic campaign by sixteen to one.**

With little money to mount an effective national advertising campaign, Bryan took to the railroads and went on a nationwide **whistle-stop campaign**. Up to that time, it was seen as unseemly for presidential candidates to actively go out and campaign for themselves, and the novelty of seeing a presidential candidate in person drew large crowds to Bryan's campaign stops. Outside of the large Eastern cities, few had ever had the chance to listen to the powerful oratory of a skillful speaker.

In the end, money won out although the election was fairly close because the South again voted solidly for the Democrat as did a few of the Western states. McKinley won by only about 600,000 votes out of almost 14 million votes cast.

The Presidential Election of 1900

The presidential election of 1900 turned out to be a rematch of the 1896 election. This time, McKinley chose New York's governor, **Theodore Roosevelt**, as his running mate. Although Roosevelt didn't want to give up his powerful position as the governor of the nation's most populous state just to be vice president, he finally relented. It was a decision that was to have significant ramifications for him and for the country.

Although Bryan again carried the South, this time, the election was not quite as close because McKinley managed to carry more of the Western states.

In 1901, during a visit to the Pan-American Exposition in Buffalo, New York, McKinley was wounded in the stomach by an assassin's bullet. A local doctor could not find the bullet, and it was assumed the president had only been grazed. Although he suffered continuing digestive problems, he soon resumed his daily duties. What was not known to the doctors was that the bullet was still lodged in his stomach and gangrene was slowly killing the president. He died on September 14, 1901, and Roosevelt rushed to Washington to assume the duties of president.

The Presidential Election of 1904

The **presidential election of 1904** saw Republican **Theodore Roosevelt** running for his first full term as president against **Alton B. Parker**, a New York Supreme Court justice. Because Roosevelt had served a good part of the prior presidents term, he promised that if he was elected he would not to seek another term.

Parker, the Democrat, was relatively unknown, and he was going up against the popular and flamboyant Roosevelt. He was only able to carry the South, which, since Lincoln, continued to vote *against* the Republicans no matter who they put up. In fact, in Florida, Louisiana, Mississippi, and South Carolina, Roosevelt was only able to get a few thousand votes despite his overwhelming popularity everywhere else in the country.

The Presidential Election of 1908

Roosevelt was true to his promise not to seek another term, so for the presidential election of 1908, the Republicans put up **William H. Taft** who was Roosevelt's Secretary of War.

The Democrats, for the third time, put up **William Jennings Bryan**. Although Bryan was by then a very experienced presidential campaigner, his campaign was under funded. He was again only able to carry the South and a few of the Western states.

Taft was elected by a comfortable margin.

The Presidential Election of 1912

The presidential election season in 1912 began with a potential European war in the background. As it turned out, it would mark the first presidential election since the ascendancy of the Republican and Democratic parties in which those two parties did not control essentially all of the Electoral College votes.

There were four serious candidates running for president in 1912. **Republican William H. Taft was** running for reelection. The **Democrats** ran **Woodrow Wilson**, the Governor of New Jersey and they chose **Thomas R. Marshall**, the governor of Indiana as his running mate. The **Socialist Party** ran **Eugene V. Debs. Theodore Roosevelt** decided to run for president again, but this time as the **Progressive Party's** candidate.

Although Roosevelt had promised not to run for reelection as president in 1908, he had a falling out with fellow Republican William Taft and decided to try to unseat him. He came in second in the voting, and in the end, all he accomplished was to help a Democrat get elected president for the first time since 1892.

Added together, Roosevelt and Taft received more votes than Wilson. However, they won only 96 Electoral College votes. Wilson received 453 Electoral College votes and was therefore elected the nation's 28th president.

Chapter Nine
The Politics of War

The Presidential Election of 1916

The **presidential election of 1916** took place against the backdrop of an ongoing bloody war in Europe. Wilson ran for reelection as a **Democrat** on a platform of keeping the U.S. out of the war. It was a popular position in 1916.

The **Republicans** put up Supreme Court Justice **Charles Evans Hughes**. He received the support of former president, Theodore Roosevelt.

The **Socialists** again put up a candidate, **A. L. Benson**, and although the socialist ideas were gaining some popularity in the country, there was little chance he would be able to win any Electoral College votes.

The popular vote was close with 9,126,868 votes going to Wilson and 8,548,728 votes going for Hughes.

The Electoral College vote was also close, but Wilson was able to prevail 277 to 254. His 23 vote majority in the Electoral College meant it would have taken only one or two states to swing the Electoral College in the other direction. In many states outside of the South, the vote was very close.

COMMENT:

Despite the ongoing war in Europe, after the election of 1916, most Americans still wanted the United States to maintain its neutrality.

However, part of Germany's war effort was to use their fleet of U-boats (submarines) to attack and sink any ship that might be bringing supplies to England.

At that time, the United States was very dependent on its trade with England and other European countries that were allied with Britain. When the U.S. tried to maintain that trade despite the war, the German U-boats began to sink U.S. ships, and President Wilson began to threaten Germany with retaliation.

At about the same time, American officials learned Germany was trying to use the memory of the Mexican-American war to get Mexico to join Germany's war effort.

When that information was published by several U.S. newspapers, Americans were outraged. Although Wilson had promised in his campaign for the presidency to keep the United States out of the war in Europe, he now went before Congress to ask for a declaration of war against Germany.

Many Americans still wanted to stay out of the war, but throughout history, few members of Congress have dared to vote against going to war if a president requests it. On April 6, 1917, the Senate voted 82 to 6 to declare war on Germany. The House followed suit and voted 373 to 50 to allow the United States to enter **World War One** against the Germans.

The Presidential Election of 1920

Leading up to the **presidential election of 1920,** there was much turmoil in the country. In the early part of the twentieth century, labor unions were gaining considerable power, and they had begun using strikes as a tactic for improving wages and working conditions. Strife over labor issues led to race riots in several parts of the country. One race riot that pitted blacks and whites against each other in East St. Louis resulted in the deaths of more than one hundred African-Americans. Another riot erupted in Chicago when Irish groups fought African-Americans who were attempting to get jobs at the Chicago stockyards.

Because the previous several elections had been close, both of the leading political parties tried to pick candidates from states with the most Electoral College votes. At that time, Ohio had 24 electoral votes, and as it turned out, both parties ended up picking candidates from that state.

The Democrats nominated Ohio Governor **James M. Cox**, and the Republicans chose Ohio Senator **Warren G. Harding**. Both had influence because both were newspaper publishers in an era when newspapers were becoming powerful political tools.

The Socialist again put up **Eugene V. Debs**, and although he was unable to win any Electoral College votes, he was able to capture almost a million popular votes.

The race between Harding and Cox did not turn out to be as close as everyone thought it would. Harding won Ohio easily, and he also won most of the other large states. Cox, the Democrat, carried all of the Southern states, but it was not enough to win.

Warren G. Harding won the Electoral College vote and became the 29th president.

In 1923, Harding died in office and his vice president, **Calvin Coolidge**, the former governor of Massachusetts, served out the last year of his term.

The Presidential Election of 1924

In the **presidential election of 1924,** Republican Coolidge, ran for reelection against Democrat **John W. Davis**, a prominent lawyer from West Virginia.

A third-party candidate, **Robert M. La Follette**, a **Progressive** from Wisconsin also ran. He was to become the most successful third-party candidate in the modern era. He won 4,831,706 votes and carried his home state of Wisconsin with its 13 Electoral College votes.

However, this time, the election was not close enough for the presence of a third party candidate to throw the decision into the House of Representatives.

Although Davis, the Democrat, once again carried the entire South, that was all he won.

Coolidge was elected with a large majority in the Electoral College.

The Presidential Election of 1928

In the **presidential election of 1928,** Coolidge chose not to run for reelection, and the Republicans nominated **Herbert Hoover** from California, He had been the nation's Commerce Secretary under president Harding. At that point in time, it was one of the few times a candidate from the West had been nominated by a major party.

The Democrats nominated Governor **Al Smith** from New York, but unfortunately for him, many voters associated him with the well-publicized Tammany Hall corruption that had been going on in New York (even though he was not part of it). In addition, Smith was a Roman Catholic, and there was a widespread belief among Protestants that, if elected, he might take orders from the Pope.

Despite Smith's religion, he was still a Democrat going up against a Republican so he won all of the Protestant South except for Florida. After 68 years, the South was still voting *against* the Republicans, the party that had elected the hated Abraham Lincoln.

Hoover easily won the presidency by one of the largest pluralities in modern presidential election history.

COMMENT:

Religion has rarely played a role in presidential elections. Up until **Roman Catholic** Al Smith was the Democratic nominee for president in 1928, every candidate had been a Protestant. After Al Smith lost badly, neither the Democrats nor the Republicans nominated another Roman Catholic until Senator John Kennedy was nominated by the Democrats in 1960 (who won in a very close election despite much discussion about his religion).

Roman Catholic Senator John Kerry was nominated by the Democrats in 2004, and he lost in a close election. This time the focus was on the Vietnam war, and there was not much discussion about religion.

There has never been a Jewish candidate nominated for president by either the Democrats or the Republicans.

The Republican nomination of Mitt Romney for president in 2012 will mark the first time either party has nominated a Mormon for president. The question is, will his religion influence voters.

If we look back to the election of 1928, it tells us something important about voters and religion. In that election, the mostly Protestant South voted *for* the Democratic Roman Catholic nominee, Al Smith. The voters of the South of that era consistently voted *against* the Republicans, no matter what candidate they put forward. Today, that trend has reversed: now the South mostly votes for the Republican candidate. Although there has been a lot of talk about Romney's Mormon religion, it seems likely that the conservative voters in the Southern states, who have been consistently voting *against* whatever candidate the Democrats nominate, will continue to do so and vote for Mitt Romney, no matter what religion he practices.

The Presidential Election of 1932

The **presidential election of 1932** took place in the middle of the Great Depression.

The Democrats nominated **Franklin D. Roosevelt**, the wealthy governor of New York. He chose John Nance Garner IV from Texas as his running mate.

The Republicans put up **Hoover** for reelection, but with the economy being in such bad shape, few gave him much of a chance to hold onto the presidency.

During the campaign, there was some talk about Roosevelt's health being an issue. Roosevelt had contracted polio in 1921 and the infection left him permanently paralyzed from the waist down. At that time, polio (poliomyelitis) was a common childhood disease and outbreaks of the disease were all too common during the summer months, especially in large cities. There was no cure at that time and there still isn't; however, a vaccine was developed, and due to a nearly universal vaccination program, the disease is rare today.

Roosevelt learned to get around a bit with the help of leg braces and canes, and at home he used a wheelchair. However, for the rest of his life, he was careful to never be seen by the public in that wheelchair. The most famous pictures of him, such as in the back seat of his convertible, or on the deck of the USS Quincy at the end of WWII, always showed him sitting down.

The election was a landslide for Roosevelt. Hoover only won six Northeastern states, Connecticut, Delaware, Maine, New Hampshire, Pennsylvania, and Vermont, and even in those states his margin of victory was very slim.

The Presidential Election of 1936

With the depression still going on, **Roosevelt** ran for reelection in 1936. His running mate was again John Garner.

The Republicans nominated **Alf Landon**, the governor of Kansas.

For the Democrats, there was some concern that Roosevelt might lose the South, and other conservative states because the Republicans were aggressively attacking him as a socialist. They claimed his "**New Deal**" policies, including Social Security and unemployment relief, were taking the United States down the road toward socialism.

But Roosevelt needn't have worried because once again, he carried every Southern state. In fact, in the Southern states where African-Americans were systematically kept from voting, the Republican candidate hardly got any votes at all. For example, in Mississippi, Landon got only 4,443 votes, and in South Carolina he only got 1,646 votes. It was clear that even 76 years after Lincoln's election, the conservative South was still voting *against* Lincoln and the Republicans, even if it meant voting for a very liberal (and some said *socialist*) candidate.

Roosevelt surprised everyone (including some pollsters) by carrying every state except Maine and Vermont. His Electoral College win was 523 to 8.

COMMENT:

The Great Depression, like all economic downturns, influenced presidential elections and presidential policy for many years. It was the main reason Hoover was overwhelmingly rejected by the voters, and it was the main reason Roosevelt was able to enact many of his new programs (most of Roosevelt's New Deal programs were attacked by the Republicans, and later some of the programs were declared unconstitutional).

Although there were some fundamental problems in the U.S. economy before 1929, the depression is usually thought to have begun on "**Black Tuesday**," October 29, 1929. That day the U.S. stock market dropped dramatically. The downturn had actually begun the week before when a smaller downturn scared some investors, and the following Monday many of them chose to get out of the market. The next day, Black Tuesday, even more investors sold out and a huge number of shares were traded. Stocks fell an average of twelve percent.

William C. Durant and **the Rockefeller family** saw the fall in stock prices as an opportunity to buy them at historically low prices, so they stepped in and bought stocks in large quantities. That helped convince some investors that the market was safe, but after a bit of recovery, the market began to fall again.

Investors like **John D. Rockefeller** tried to talk about a stock market comeback, but many ordinary citizens had begun to invest in the market, and they had lost money in the downturn. In order to attract investors, stock brokers were in the habit of lending small investors money to buy stocks, so it was not just stock speculators that were wiped out. Many people reacted to the decreasing stock values by taking their money out of the stock market, *and* they began to spend less to make up for their losses. That started a cycle of business slowdown and job layoffs, which led to even less spending.

It didn't help that the Midwestern plains states were suffering from an extended drought that eventually led to what was referred to as the "**dust bowl**" (the drying out and blowing away of rich agricultural soil).

President Hoover's response to the economic slowdown was to try to pressure businesses to keep workers employed and to keep wages high. That didn't work very well because the businesses were under too much pressure from decreasing sales. Hoover did lower some taxes, but at first he was opposed to the government getting involved in job programs or putting money into the economy in any other way. Instead, he believed churches and private charities should take up the challenge. As for government back-to-work programs, he said that was up to local and state governments.

When the depression worsened, Hoover *did* begin to institute some large-scale government job-creation programs. The huge Hoover Dam project on the Colorado River is one example.

As the 1932 election approached, many U.S. citizens blamed the economic downturn on Hoover, and whether or not that was a fair judgment, it led to his loss to Franklin Roosevelt.

The Presidential Election of 1940

By the time the presidential election of 1940 came around, the economy was improving and all attention was on the war in Europe. The country was divided as to whether the U.S. should go to the aid of England and France.

John Garner, Roosevelt's vice president, assumed Roosevelt would stick to tradition and not run for a third term, so he decided to make a run for the presidency on the Democratic ticket. He was much more conservative than Roosevelt and disagreed with much of the New Deal agenda. As a result, he had much wider support in the South and in the conservative rural states.

However, Democratic President Roosevelt soon decided to break with tradition and run for a third term. He chose his Secretary of Commerce, **Henry Wallace** from Iowa.

After the Republicans were unable to agree on a candidate, a surprising dark horse named **Wendell Willkie** came forward. He was an industrialist from Indiana who had never been much involved in politics.

Throughout the election, the Republicans focused on Roosevelt's perceived failure to end the depression and his apparent willingness to get the United States involved in the ongoing war in Europe.

Roosevelt responded by saying it was his New Deal programs that were ending the Great Depression, and he said he had no intention of getting involved in the European war.

Again, there was talk that Roosevelt was too liberal, and that meant he would lose the conservative South.

In 1940, it did seem possible that a Republican could win the South because a "conservative coalition" had emerged in Congress that brought together conservative Southern Democrats with conservative Republicans. By election time, they had already been successful at defeating *some* of Roosevelt's liberal New Deal policies. Many thought the two groups would work together to defeat Roosevelt in the upcoming presidential election.

However, it didn't work out that way. The citizens of the South continued to vote straight Democratic. They were still unwilling to vote for the hated "Lincoln-Republicans," no matter how liberal Roosevelt was.

The East also went for Roosevelt, except once again, conservative Maine and Vermont voted against him.

COMMENT:

When Franklin D. Roosevelt ran for an unprecedented third term, and again when he ran for a fourth term, the Republicans pointed out the fact that George Washington had declined to run for a third term as president. They said President Washington's decision indicated the founding fathers had wanted to limit the time a president could serve.

Based on that reasoning, they introduced a measure to amend the Constitution to limit the number of terms a person could hold the presidency. It was passed and the result was the Twenty-Second Amendment which limited any one individual's term of presidency to two terms. It was ratified by three-fourths of the states on February 27, 1951.

The Presidential Election of 1944

By the time the presidential election of 1944 came around, the nation was at war. Germany's ally, **the Japanese, had attacked the U.S. naval base at Pearl Harbor in Hawaii** and it immediately drew the United States into **World War Two**.

As the fall election approached, the entire country was focused on winning what was turning out to be a very difficult war.

Every family had somebody involved "over there" and casualties were high. Most of the families in America dreaded the arrival of the telegraph man, sure that any news from Europe would be bad news.

In addition, nearly every family in the country was either working on something related to the war effort, or suffering restrictions because of it. Although the war was taking place far away, there was a feeling that if the Germans and the Japanese were not stopped "over there," they would soon arrive on our shores. As a result, the people were probably less involved in the election of 1944 than any previous election.

For the 1944 presidential election, the **Republicans** put up **Thomas E. Dewey**, the governor of New York. He chose **John Bricker**, the Governor of Ohio, as his running mate.

It was no surprise when **Roosevelt ran for reelection in 1944**, this time with Harry S. Truman as his vice president. With the U.S. in the middle of a war, most thought he would be reelected.

Dewey campaigned hard against Roosevelt, saying four terms for a president was too many. Some accused the president of trying to become a king. Others continued to **try to paint him as a socialist**, pointing out that some of his New Deal programs had been declared unconstitutional, and others had been overturned in Congress (mostly through the efforts of the conservative coalition).

By the time the election campaign was underway, the economy was improving, helping Roosevelt's chances. In addition, U.S. troops had landed on the beaches of Normandy on June 6, 1944, and although American casualties were heavy, the invasion was a success. Within days, U.S. troops were pushing inland in France.

By the end of August, U.S. troops were in Paris, and there had been a string of successful battles against Japan in the Pacific. By election day, U.S. troops were at the Germany border.

The military successes of that summer were enough to convince most U.S. citizens that Roosevelt was running the war properly .

Roosevelt was reelected for a fourth term, again winning all of the Southern states. However, much of the conservative Midwest voted against Roosevelt, and Dewey, the Republican candidate, actually got quite a few votes in some of the Southern states. The conservative versus liberal message was beginning to gain some traction in the South. For example, although Roosevelt won North Carolina, Dewey managed to get 263,155 votes. In West Virginia, where Roosevelt had won easily in 1940, Dewey got 322,819 votes.

However, in the deep South, the people had still not forgiven the Republicans for electing Lincoln. They still voted for the Democrat, no matter who he was. And although Roosevelt had nearly unanimous support among the large African-American population in the South, there were still restriction in place to try to keep them from voting.

The people of the South that were allowed to vote voted for the liberal Democrat Roosevelt in overwhelm numbers. For example, in Mississippi, Dewey only got 11,601 votes.

Nationwide, the popular vote was fairly close, 25,612,916 for Roosevelt and 22,017,929 for Dewey. But the Electoral College vote was not close. It came out 432 for Roosevelt and only 99 for Dewey.

Roosevelt died after only a few months into his fourth term. His vice president, **Harry Truman,** was sworn in as president, and he presided over the last few months of the war, including the atomic bomb attacks on Japan.

COMMENT:

World War Two did not play as much of a role in U.S. presidential politics as you might think. Although the war did influence the voting that took place prior to the election of 1940 when Wendell Willkie accused Roosevelt of trying to get the U.S involved in what they saw as a European war, Roosevelt's promise to keep the country out of the war defused Willkie's attack.

But when Japan attacked the American naval base at Pearl Harbor, nearly all Americans supported Roosevelt when he went on the radio to tell the country he had asked Congress for a declaration of war on Japan. **His "day of infamy" speech** was a rallying cry for the U.S. to enter the war on the side of the allies. He issued a presidential order that said any government agency that was in any way related to the war effort would report directly him. He ordered many corporations to modify their manufacturing lines to make war materials and established a goal of producing 10,000 new fighter airplanes per year. He also ordered an emergency shipbuilding program to quickly build ships to carry troops and war material.

The **Selective Service Act** was passed with Roosevelt's help, and when the U.S. declared war on Japan and Germany, all men in the United States between the ages of 16 to 65 were required to register for the draft.

Millions of young men were drafted into the Army and millions more voluntarily signed up to serve in one of the military branches.

It is a little known fact that the Selective Service Act even provided a role for those who were, for reasons of religion or personal belief, unwilling to fight in wars. It said they would not be required to undergo combat training but would instead undergo training for noncombatant support roles.

America's isolationist stance had left the country unprepared to fight a war, but once war was declared, most citizens were willing to make sacrifices to help. In 1944, most people felt that included supporting and voting for President Roosevelt.

The Presidential Election of 1948

In 1948, Truman ran for reelection. He was nominated by the Democrats, and he chose U.S. Senator **Alben Barkley** as his running mate.

The Republicans again nominated **Thomas Dewey** and his running mate, Earl Warren, the Governor of California.

Henry A. Wallace, Roosevelt's former vice president, was also on the ballot as a **Progressive Party** candidate.

Despite the national joy that the war was finally over, Truman was not popular. There was trouble brewing in Asia and elsewhere as an aftermath of the war, and there was some unease about the fact that Truman had ordered atomic bombs dropped on innocent Japanese civilians when many thought the war was all but over anyhow. There was also concern about what was going on in Europe. The division of Berlin between the Eastern and Western powers was still unsettled, and Russia's blockade of Berlin was an indication of the cold war that would develop between Russia and the United States.

There was also the first signs that the South was no longer going to just blindly vote for Democrats.

At the Democratic national nominating convention, Truman had promised to introduce **civil rights legislation**. Hearing that, the Southern Democratic delegates all got up and walked out. They held their own convention in Birmingham, Alabama and nominated Senator Strom Thurmond from South Carolina as a **States' Right Democrat**.

Thurmond ran on a segregationist platform and managed to squeak out wins in Alabama and Louisiana. He won his home state of South Carolina and he won Mississippi overwhelmingly.

The first results showed the election was very close. Truman had lost *some* of the South, *some* of the Midwest, but he won the Northeast and the West coast.

Some newspapers came out the morning after the election with mistaken banner headlines declaring "**Dewey Wins**," but when the long process of counting of ballots was finally finished, Truman had won after all with 24,179,347 nationwide popular votes over Dewey's 21,991,292 votes.

The final Electoral College vote was Truman 303, Dewey 189, and Thurmond 39.

Thurmond's wins in the South marked the first time in the modern era that a third-party candidate had won a significant number of electoral votes. Had the election in the northern states been closer, it would have thrown the decision about who would be president into the House of Representatives.

Chapter Ten
Postwar and Cold War Politics

The Presidential Election of 1952

In 1952, the Republicans finally managed to convince **World War Two hero**, General **Dwight D. Eisenhower**, to run for president. They had tried to convince him to run in 1948, but he had refused. This time they told him it was his duty to the country, and he finally accepted. Because the **Cold War** with Russia was bound to be one of the main election issues, he chose noted anti-communist, **Richard Nixon** from California, as his running mate.

The Democrats were in a quandary because Truman, the incumbent, had decided not to run. By 1952, primary elections to select a party's candidate were becoming the norm and in the Democratic primaries, Governor **Adlai Stevenson II** of Illinois was showing well. He was nominated at the 1952 Democratic national presidential nominating convention in Chicago. In an attempt to recapture the Southern vote, he selected **John Jackson Sparkman from Alabama** as his running mate.

There was little doubt about the popularity of General Eisenhower, but some of his opinions were very controversial. He was a strong believer in the United Nations, and thought that organization could better control the expansion of nuclear weapons than the United States could. Those kinds of non-nationalistic opinions were strongly opposed by **Republican Senator Joseph McCarthy** who was beating the drums of nationalism and stirring up anti-communist "witch hunts" through the use of his congressional committee that was finding anti-American communist spies under every rock. He said there were "commies" everywhere, including, he said, within the entertainment industry and even deep inside the U.S. government.

Two years before, the **Korean War** had flared up as a result of the postwar division of that country. The conflict was showing signs of expanding into a showdown with China, and maybe even Russia. This time the people of the United States were not so enthusiastic about getting involved in another war because they were still recovering from the depravation and losses in Second World War.

By 1952, Russia had developed its own atomic bomb, and Joseph Stalin, the Russian Premier was making threatening comments toward the U.S. In the face of such threats, what the United States needed was a hero. Eisenhower, the famous General, fit that bill. He was elected by a large majority in the Electoral College, 442 to 89, to be the first Republican in the White House in 20 years.

As usual, the South mostly went to the Democrats. Stevenson won most of the Southern states by large majorities. However, for the first time in many years, a few Southern states, Florida, Tennessee, and Virginia, went for the Republican candidate, although by narrow majorities in each case. After 92 years, cracks in the anti-Lincoln, anti-Republican Southern attitude were beginning to show.

COMMENT:

The **Korean War** was one of the Asian conflicts that flared up after World War Two over who would control a country after the Japanese were forced to withdraw.

Without consulting the Koreans, the allies decided to divide the country north and south. In 1950, armed conflict broke out between the divided sections.

As the conflict escalated, the North Koreans were supported by the People's Republic of China and Russia (the Union of Soviet Socialist Republics), while the South Koreans were being supported by the United States. It was to become the first armed conflict of the so-called "**cold war**" that pitted the U.S. against what was seen as a communist agenda to control the post-war world. From the U.S. point of view, the "war" was mostly against Russia, but there was also talk about a threat from communist China.

With the support of the U.S. military, the South Koreans invaded the North, only to be pushed back when the Chinese army came to the aid of the North Koreans.

In 1953, an uneasy stalemate was reached along the 38th parallel that divided the country north and south. A **Demilitarized Zone** along that line still maintains the stalemate to this day. Democratic South Korea has developed a thriving economy based on manufacturing and export, while North Korea has retreated into a secretive communist dictatorship which has, reportedly, pushed most of its citizens into poverty. Nevertheless, many South Koreans still hope for eventual unification.

The Presidential Election of 1956

In 1956, **Eisenhower** again ran against **Adlai Stevenson**.

The cold war was still going on, but Senator McCarthy had been discredited leaving most Americans less worried about communist infiltration here at home. Nevertheless, despite the country being in a period of peace and prosperity, the U.S. military was actively pursuing development of every more powerful nuclear weapons in response to a perceived threat from Russia that was doing the same.

With the Korean War becoming only a memory, and the U.S. economy doing well, Eisenhower was assured another term. He won every state outside of the South, and even there he picked up a few more states than in the previous election, squeaking out wins in Kentucky and West Virginia. However, Eisenhower was soundly beaten by Stevenson in the traditionally anti-Republican states of Mississippi and South Carolina.

Despite the strength of the Democratic Party in the South, voters were beginning to rebel. The South had a long history of voting *against* the Republican candidate no matter who he was, but many Southern voters were starting to resist voting for Democratic candidates they saw as Northern liberals who were threatening to pass new legislation to break down the Southern policy of strict segregation and give African-Americans more civil rights. In the 1956 election, some

Southern Democratic leaders broke with the national Democratic Party and tried to manipulate the Electoral College outcome by getting a slate of "**unpledged**" electors onto the ballot. (An unpledged elector has not pledged to support any particular candidate for President.) With unpledged electors on the ballot, voters could register their displeasure with the Democratic Party's candidate, in this case, Adlai Stevenson.

In Alabama, the unpledged electors got 20,150 votes. In Louisiana, they got 44,520 votes. In Mississippi, they got 42,266 votes (seventeen percent of the total vote), and in South Carolina, they got 88,509 votes (almost thirty percent of the total vote). In fact, in South Carolina, although Stevenson won, the unpledged electors got more votes than Eisenhower. It was clear voting patterns were changing in the South. Although the unpledged electors were unable to win any states, it was a sign of things to come in the South.

For the first time, political television advertising played a significant role in a presidential election, with much of the TV advertising aimed at women voters.

The Presidential Election of 1960

In 1960, Eisenhower's vice president, Californian **Richard Nixon**, was nominated by the Republicans to run against the Democratic nominee, **John F. Kennedy,** the young senator from Massachusetts.

From the beginning, everyone knew it was going to be a close election. The economy was not doing all that well, and the Russian launch of the world's first satellite, Sputnik, gave Americans the feeling that the U.S. was falling behind.

There was even talk that the election would end up in the House of Representatives because there was a movement underway in the South to take votes away from Kennedy who was seen as too liberal and very likely to introduce legislation that would outlaw segregation and end discrimination against African-Americans.

Nixon, despite having served as vice president under the fairly liberal Eisenhower, was known as a conservative. Many thought he would be a more appealing candidate for Southern voters. People speculated that the Democratic Party's hold on the South was about to end, which would dramatically change future American presidential elections.

The **1960 election introduced televised debates** leading many to speculate that the election would be won or lost by how well the candidates came across on the small screen. Analysis of the four televised debates revealed an odd fact: those who heard the debates on the radio thought Nixon did very well, but those who watched the debates on television thought he did very poorly against the calm and polished Kennedy. It was becoming clear that television was going to be the way people learned about the candidates.

By the election of 1960, Alaska and Hawaii had been admitted to the Union and the citizens of the two newest states would finally be able to participate in a presidential election. However, with only six electoral votes between them, they didn't get much attention from the candidates.

The real election battleground was in the South. To help him win the Southern States, Kennedy chose **Texan Lyndon B. Johnson** as his running mate.

Despite much negative talk about Kennedy being a Catholic, he held onto the predominantly Protestant Southern states of Georgia, Louisiana, North Carolina, and South Carolina. But the emerging conservative movement in the South cost him Florida, Kentucky, Tennessee, and Virginia.

The conservatives managed to elect a slate of unpledged electors in Mississippi. In fact, in that state, the unpledged electors received more votes than either Nixon or Kennedy. Therefore, they won all eight of that state's electoral votes. In Alabama, Nixon received more votes than Kennedy, but the majority of the state's voters voted for the six unpledged conservative electors who, it was clear, were not going to cast their Electoral College votes for either Kennedy or Nixon.

When the Electoral College met to cast their ballots, all of the unpledged electors cast their votes for segregationists Harry F. Byrd and Strom Thurmond.

Nevertheless, Kennedy managed to win enough Electoral College votes to be elected president. The final Electoral College vote was Kennedy 303, Nixon 219, and Harry Byrd 15.

COMMENT:

As in most close elections, there were accusations of voter fraud in favor of Kennedy, especially in Mayor Daley's Chicago, and in Johnson's home state of Texas. Investigators later found that in some counties in Texas, more votes were cast for the Kennedy-Johnson ticket than there were voters in that county.

As soon as Kennedy was elected, he instituted new domestic programs and set about to change the nation's foreign policy. At home, he reinvigorated the space program and promised a balanced budget.

The Republicans, said Kennedy was soft on communism, but in the spring of 1961, he authorized a plan to try to overthrow the communist government of Cuba. The CIA and the U.S. military landed 1500 former Cubans near the **Bay of Pigs** on the remote south side of the island of Cuba. They had been trained by the U.S. military in guerrilla tactics and were supposed to rally the people against Fidel Castro's government. However, the Cuban military soon killed or rounded up all of the guerrillas, and the U.S. was forced to pay a ransom to get the survivors back.

Then, in October of 1962, CIA U-2 spy planes photographed missile sites being built by Russian technicians in Cuba. It was possible the missiles could be used in a future nuclear attack on the United States.

It was the greatest crisis of Kennedy's administration. The military wanted to immediately bomb the missile sites, but Kennedy was afraid that would lead to a direct confrontation with Russia, with the potential that it could escalate into nuclear war.

Kennedy decided on a naval blockade of Cuba until the missiles were removed.

Tension with Russia mounted until a deal was secretly struck. Russia's Premier, Nikita Khrushchev, agreed to dismantle the missile sites in Cuba if the U.S. would dismantle its missile sites in Turkey and promise never to invade Cuba. Kennedy agreed.

The "**Cuban Missile Crisis**" as it came to be known, quieted Republican criticism of Kennedy as being soft on communism and considerably enhanced Kennedy's approval rating.

In November of 1963, President Kennedy was on a visit to Dallas. He was riding in the back seat of a convertible limousine when he was shot and killed by Lee Harvey Oswald, a former Marine marksman who had positioned himself above the street in a 6th floor window of a nearby building.

Lyndon Johnson was immediately sworn in as president to serve out the last year of the presidency before the election of 1964.

Chapter Eleven
The Politics of War and Antiwar

The Presidential Election of 1964

In 1964, sitting president **Lyndon Johnson** was nominated for reelection by the **Democrats**.

In 1964, Johnson's only serious competition in those primaries came from **Alabama's governor George Wallace** who had come to national prominence when he stood in the doorway of the University of Alabama to block the entrance of black students. The event was covered on live TV.

Wallace's name appeared on three of the sixteen states that were holding Democratic presidential primaries that year, Wisconsin, Indiana, and Maryland. Running on a segregationist platform, Wallace won a surprising number of votes in those states.

COMMENT:

George Wallace's infamous "**stand in the schoolhouse door**" came about after the United States Supreme Court handed down a decision that state taxpayer-supported universities could not legally refuse to admit students because of their race. Most states complied to one degree or another, but the University of Alabama, with the support of the state's governor and other leading politicians, found ways to reject a student application if they found out the student had *any* African-American heritage.

When the University of Alabama refused to accept the applications of three fully-qualified African-American students, the students went to court. A federal judge ordered them to be admitted.

> When the three student arrived on the opening day of classes, Governor Wallace was there in the doorway with local police to block their entrance. He had made sure there would be plenty of news media present to record the confrontation, and the national TV networks carried the event live for all the nation to watch.
>
> Knowing ahead of time what was going to happen, President Kennedy federalized the Alabama National Guard and ordered them to make sure the students were admitted, by force if necessary.
>
> The students were admitted, but it gained Wallace a big following throughout the South and that emboldened him to make a run for the presidency of the United States.

Despite Wallace's presence in the race, at the Democratic national nominating convention, Johnson won easily. He chose U.S. Senator **Hubert Humphrey** from Minnesota as his running mate.

The Republicans nominated **Barry Goldwater**, a conservative from Arizona. He chose Congressman **William E. Miller** from New York as his running mate.

Continuing the trend started in 1960, the candidates primarily used television to get their message across to the public. In the presidential election of 1964, television "attack" ads began to evolve into to the unrelenting barrage of attack ads we see in today's political campaigns.

Johnson's ads used skillfully done movie-like scenarios to portray what might happen if Goldwater was elected. The infamous "**Daisy Girl**" **ad** showed an innocent-looking little girl picking petals from a daisy in a field of flowers. As she counted the flower's petals, the screen morphed into a missile launch countdown followed by a dramatic nuclear explosion. The ads were in response to Goldwater's statement that nuclear weapons might have to be used in some circumstances. Although it didn't come right out and accuse Goldwater of being an advocate of nuclear war, the ad effectively made the point that Goldwater's opinions could lead the country in that dangerous direction.

By 1964, the conservative wing of the Republicans was gaining control of the party. They turned away from Nixon because he was seen as too liberal, and instead chose conservative Senator **Barry Goldwater.** Governor Nelson Rockefeller of New York made a bid for the Republican nomination, but he too was seen as politically too moderate.

The 1964 presidential election gave the people a clear choice. They could vote for the outspokenly conservative and anti-communist Goldwater, or the avowed liberal Johnson who wanted to create a "great society" through government policy.

Through television advertising, Johnson was able to paint Goldwater as a dangerous anti-communist radical who might get the U.S. into a direct conflict with the Russians.

Paradoxically, Johnson was already secretly getting the country more deeply involved in the cold war against the communists. As the election campaign progressed, U.S. forces were beginning to engage enemy forces in Vietnam. President Johnson was fully aware of the worsening situation there, but he didn't want the war to be at the forefront of the American public's attention with the election coming up.

Johnson won most of the nation in a landslide, but Goldwater carried Alabama, Georgia, Louisiana, Mississippi, and South Carolina. It was the first time a Republican had carried that much of the deep South, and it marked the end of a one hundred year dominance of Democrats in the region. That change in voting preferences was to have a profound effect on every presidential election from then on.

COMMENT:

By the time Johnson won the election in the fall of 1964, **U.S. forces were secretly becoming more engaged in combat in Vietnam.**

Years before, President Eisenhower had told President Kennedy that he believed the U.S. would end up having to send troops to Vietnam. After soviet Premier Nikita Khrushchev said Russia would support the North Vietnamese communists, Eisenhower predicted Vietnam would be the next hot spot in the escalating "cold war."

In 1961, Johnson, as vice president, had visited President Diem in South Vietnam and hailed him as the "Winston Churchill of Asia."

Soon after that visit, skirmishes with troops from North Vietnam began. In response, President Kennedy sent a few hundred Green Beret "'advisors" to South Vietnam to help train the South Vietnamese Army.

When more attacks on South Vietnam came from the north, Vietnamese President Diem requested more military aid from Kennedy. In response, Kennedy sent General Maxwell Taylor to Vietnam to access the situation. Taylor came back alarmed at what he had seen and told Kennedy that if Vietnam fell into the hands of the communists, all of Southeast Asia would eventually fall.

The Pentagon advised Kennedy's Defense Secretary Robert McNamara that a massive show of force was needed. McNamara concurred and suggested to Kennedy that the U.S. should send at least 20,000 troops to Vietnam. Kennedy decided against it, and to this day there is discussion about whether the U.S. would have gotten so deeply involved in Vietnam had Kennedy not been assassinated.

Kennedy *did* continue to send advisors to Vietnam (eventually more than 16,000), and he also sent helicopter units. In the fall of 1961, he guaranteed President Diem that the United States would help Vietnam "preserve its independence."

In 1962, a reporter asked President Kennedy if any Americans in Vietnam were engaged in the fighting there. The president said no, but in fact, they were. U.S. pilots were participating in bombing runs using U.S. aircraft. Some of the bomb attacks were resulting in civilian causalities, and after seeing American planes doing the bombing, many South Vietnamese blamed the Americans.

Defense Secretary McNamara visited South Vietnam during the summer of 1962 and came back to tell President Kennedy that the South Vietnamese war against the northern invaders was going well because of U.S. help.

Soon after that visit, the first U.S. Special Forces base was secretly established at Khe Sanh.

When Buddhists rioters in South Vietnam took to the streets in Saigon to protest a government crackdown on religion, they were fired on by South Vietnamese troops. Several Buddhist monks publicly burned themselves to death as an act of protest.

The worldwide publicity from those acts brought Vietnam to the attention of American citizens for the first time. Some citizen groups began asking what we were doing over there, and reports began to circulate that the U.S. was supporting a corrupt government in Vietnam.

Soon, a coup was mounted against President Diem, resulting in the assassination of Diem and his brother. Later evidence showed that the CIA had at least tacitly supported the coup.

By the time Kennedy was assassinated in November 24, 1963, the situation in Vietnam was becoming very unstable. Viet Cong guerrillas were occupying more and more of the countryside.

As soon as President Johnson was sworn in, he took over management of the war. At press conferences, he began making strong statements that the U.S. would not allow the communists to take Vietnam.

At first, President Johnson made sure most of the U.S. involvement in the Vietnam War was being done covertly. Secret U.S. bombing raids, using U.S. airplanes and "volunteer" American pilots, were attacking Viet Cong bases both in Vietnam and in Laos.

Defense Secretary McNamara began making more and more public statements indicating that the U.S. would support the new Vietnamese military government. He said, "We'll stay for as long as it takes."

After that, America was committed. Johnson believed the reputation of the U.S. (and his personal reputation) was on the line.

But when word leaked out that our "support" of the South Vietnamese was already costing the U.S. more than two million dollars a day, more people began to ask if it was such a good idea to be committing those kinds of resources in a tiny and relatively unknown country half way around the world.

Johnson continued to try to keep the war low profile, mainly because he knew he didn't have the support in Congress for another Asian war so soon after the debacle in Korea.

He mostly used the CIA to conduct secret operations out of Saigon, and he used U.S. Navy warships to harass North Vietnamese installations along the coast.

Meanwhile, in Vietnam, the increasing successes of the Viet Cong were causing political instability. In one year, South Vietnam saw five different governments come into power.

In the summer of 1964, President Johnson was preoccupied with running for election. He named Lt. Gen William C. Westmoreland to oversee operations in Vietnam.

Senator Barry Goldwater, Johnson's very conservative Republican opponent in the election, was trying to use the lack of more aggressive action in Vietnam to paint Johnson as soft on communism.

At the beginning of August, only a few months before the presidential election was to take place, the **"Gulf of Tonkin Incident"** took place. It involved U.S. war ships that were supporting South Vietnamese speed boats that were staging attacks on North Vietnamese coastal installations. North Vietnamese torpedo boats came out to respond and were shelled by the USS Maddox, a Sumner-class destroyer. It was reported that at least one of the torpedo boats fired back, and that one 14.5 mm round hit the destroyer. The round didn't cause any serious damage on the Maddox, and no one was injured. Later that same day, a second attack was reported.

As minor as the incident had been, it was nevertheless the excuse Johnson had been looking for to show he was not soft on communism. He went on the radio to describe two attacks by North Vietnamese vessels against U.S. Navy ships "on the high seas." In his speech, he did not indicate that the U.S. was already involved in Vietnam in any way other than in a supporting role. The implication of his speech was that the North Vietnamese had launched an unprovoked attack on a U.S. ship that was just minding its own business out in international waters.

The truth, as we later learned, was that **neither Johnson nor McNamara were sure there really had been an attack**, and later the captain of one of the ships involved said the second attack might have actually been a false radar image.

There was some resistance in Congress to getting involved in yet another Asian war, but after some deliberation they passed the **Tonkin Gulf Resolution** which authorized President Johnson to use "conventional" military force in Southeast Asia. Significantly, it was not a formal declaration of war by Congress. The "Vietnam War" was actually termed a **"police action."** Looking back, "police action" is an odd euphemism for a conflict that is estimated to have **cost the lives of 266,000 Army of the Republic of Vietnam soldiers, 1,100,000 North Vietnamese Army and Viet Cong soldiers, 58,272 American soldiers, and 843,000 Vietnamese civilians.** In addition, **303,644 American soldiers were wounded in action** -- not counting those that suffered from **post-traumatic stress disorder (PTSD)** as a result of what they experienced in Vietnam.

As the war was escalated, there were a few protests against it back home in the U.S. However, as the news media began sending back horrific reports about what was going on over there, often showing footage of the actual fighting on the nightly TV news, the protests increased. Eventually, some of the antiwar protests attracted as many as half a million people.

The **Viet Cong's Tet offensive** in January of 1968 further undermined U.S. support for the war. Popular CBS anchorman Walter Cronkite went on TV to say that in his opinion the U.S. was mired in an unwinnable stalemate in Vietnam.

On March 31, 1968, President Johnson went on live television to announce that he would not seek reelection, saying, "There is division in the American house now."

His 1964 campaign promise of creating a "great society" had been ruined when his focus turned to combating communism,

> causing him to escalate a pointless war in Vietnam that ended in complete failure. By the end of his presidency, there was no great society, only a divided nation that was deeply involved in a war that was costing the country untold amounts of money and many thousands of American lives.

The Presidential Election of 1968

In 1968, Johnson's decision not to run for reelection meant the 1968 race for the presidency would be wide open. Everyone knew the election would be a referendum on the Vietnam War.

Richard Nixon, Eisenhower's former vice president threw his hat into the ring. His two main rivals were Michigan Governor George W. Romney (Mitt Romney's father) and California Governor Ronald Reagan.

There were clear choices between the candidates. Nixon and Reagan were both saying America had to be tough on communism, and Vietnam was a key test of America's resolve.

Romney had voted for the **Tonkin Gulf Resolution,** and he had been an early supporter of the war. But now he said Vietnam was a mistake. He said he had been "brainwashed" by the military into supporting the Vietnam War. That remark cost him votes in the Republican primaries.

Both Nixon and Reagan knew the Democrats were likely to run somebody who would make ending the Vietnam War a priority. In order to make the election about fighting communism, Nixon and Reagan tried to show they would be tougher on communism, and that they would win the war in Vietnam. Much of Nixon's oratory was to rail against the anti-war protesters that he characterized as un-American supporters of worldwide communism.

By the end of the Republican primaries, it was clear Republican voters were responding to Nixon's pro-war, anti-communist message.

There were a few antiwar protests at the **Republican national presidential nominating convention**, but most of the Republicans in attendance were in favor of continuing what they saw as a fight against communist aggression.

Nixon was nominated and as part of the new Republican "**Southern strategy**," he selected Maryland Governor Spiro Agnew as his running mate.

The **Democratic national presidential nominating convention** was anything but peaceful. Held in Chicago, it attracted many thousands of antiwar protesters who gathered outside the convention center. Mayor Richard Daley brought in 23,000 police and National Guardsmen to control the situation, and many of the protesters were beaten and arrested. Unfortunately for the Democrats, all this was shown on live TV, disrupting the coverage of the convention and making the Democrats, or at least the Chicago police, seem unnecessarily cruel. The **Walker Report**, a federal investigation of what happened, characterized it as "a police riot." The report blamed Mayor Richard J. Daley for what it called "unrestrained and indiscriminate police violence."

The assassinations of the leading Democratic presidential candidate, Senator Robert F. Kennedy, and civil rights leader, Martin Luther King, were on everybody's mind, and because of the ongoing Vietnam war, the convention was very divisive.

Hubert Humphrey, Johnson's vice president from Minnesota had won the most votes n the primaries, but after leading Democratic presidential candidate, **Robert Kennedy**, was assassinated, Senator **Eugene McCarthy**, an antiwar candidate from Minnesota, began to get a lot of votes.

Despite the divisive nature of the convention, Humphrey easily won the vote for nomination. Surprisingly, instead of picking a Southerner as his running mate, he picked **Edmund Muskie**, U.S. Senator from Maine.

The 1968 presidential election took place in an atmosphere of ongoing antiwar protests. Although Nixon worked hard to get Southern votes by appealing to conservatives, the segregationist Alabama Governor **George Wallace** managed to get himself on the ballot in the Southern states as the presidential nominee of the **American Independent Party**. He chose the outspokenly militaristic Air Force General **Curtis LeMay** as his running mate.

Wallace's main election strategy was to try to get enough Electoral College votes in Southern states to send the decision to the U.S. House of Representatives. He aggressively campaigned against the anti-segregation policies of Johnson and his vice president, Hubert Humphrey.

Wallace pledged an immediate withdrawal of U.S. troops from Vietnam. He made sure nobody thought he supported the antiwar protesters. Far from it; he said he was simply against the waste of money and lives in a pointless war in faraway Asia (which, of course, was exactly what most of the antiwar protesters were saying).

During the election, his running mate Curtis LeMay got a lot of attention by saying he did not fear using nuclear weapons in the fight against communism. He was widely quoted when he said the U.S. had the capability to **bomb Vietnam "back into the stone age**."

In the general election, Nixon's "Southern strategy" failed to win very many Southern states, mainly because of the strong showing of third-party candidate, George Wallace. But Nixon was able to get enough votes in the Midwest and West to win the election, even squeaking out a win in his usually-Democratic home state of California.

The national popular vote was one of the closest ever, 43.42% of the popular vote going to Nixon and 42.72% going to Humphrey. 31,783,783 votes were cast for Nixon, 31,271,839 went to Humphrey, and 9,901,118 went to Wallace. In the Electoral College, Nixon won 301 votes to Humphrey's 191.

Nixon's seemingly contradictory message of being *for* the war and against the antiwar protesters, and at the same time promising to somehow *end* the war with honor, had resonated with the American people.

Many observers felt Humphrey had lost a lot of votes because he didn't try hard enough to dissociate himself from Johnson's failed Vietnam policy. In addition, he had failed to follow through with the Democrat's "Southern strategy" to win votes in South by supporting some of their demands.

With two Northerners running on the Democratic ticket, **Wallace** was able to get 46 Electoral College votes in the South. His strategy of getting enough electoral votes to deny either Nixon or Humphrey the majority and send the decision to the House of Representatives failed, but it would have worked if Humphrey could have accumulated more votes in the West and in the South to make the race closer.

To his credit, Humphrey refused to pander to the South by playing down his plan to pass more civil rights legislation, and he also refused to select a vice presidential candidate from the South. Those changes in strategy might have been enough to take at least some of Wallace's votes in the South and give Humphrey the win (in Georgia, for example, Humphrey lost to Nixon by only 45,671 vote while Wallace got 535,550 votes there). If Humphrey could had won a few of the Southern states the Democrats had always won, he would have won the presidency. Wallace role as a spoiler shows that a third-party candidate can have a dramatic effect on the outcome of the presidential race. As we shall see when we look at the presidential election of 2000, a third-party candidate can even deny the presidency to the popular vote winner.

COMMENT:

It didn't take Nixon long to grab hold of the same "**Vietnam tar baby**" that had ruined Johnson's presidency. By the time Nixon entered the White House, over 500,000 troops were stationed in Vietnam and **American soldiers were dying at the rate of 1200 a month**. With the antiwar protests mounting and public opinion turning against the war, many expected Nixon to began to de-escalate U.S. involvement there. But he did not. In fact, he escalated it.

The new Secretary of State, Henry Kissinger had convinced Nixon that the war was not "winnable" in the traditional sense, but Nixon knew withdrawal would be political suicide. He had been elected to "win" the war in Vietnam and to win it "with honor." That meant military victory in Vietnam was mandatory.

Nixon and Kissinger came up with a two part strategy: they would build up South Vietnam's military to get them to take over more of the actual combat. At the same time, Nixon would order an increase in the intensity of the war in hopes it would bring the North Vietnamese to the bargaining table.

Nixon ordered increased bombing of North Vietnam, including civilian areas. And he **ordered U.S. troops into the neighboring neutral countries** of Cambodia and Laos.

Meanwhile, at home, Nixon tried to paint anti-war groups as supporters of communism. Even as the antiwar protests grew, he tried to appeal to the "silent majority," the majority of Americans he said were quietly supporting what he was doing in Vietnam. He tried to paint anyone who disagreed with him as radical communist sympathizers. He also railed against the "liberal media," saying most of their news items about him were distorted, manufactured attempts to discredit him.

Meanwhile, the antiwar protests increased. In response to the protests at Kent State University in Ohio, the governor of Ohio, James Rhodes, sent in the National Guard with live ammunition in their rifles. On Monday, May 4, 1970, members of the National Guard fired into a crowd of students. Thirteen students were hit, and four died. Some of the students who were killed were shot intentionally as they tried to run away, but other students were killed some distance away as they were walking to their classes.

When the details of the killings at Kent State were reported, many American Universities were shut down in sympathy.

Even though a presidential commission harshly criticized the guardsmen, concluding that "the indiscriminate firing of rifles into a crowd of students and the deaths that followed were unnecessary, unwarranted, and inexcusable," the killings dramatically increased the popularity of Governor Rhodes in Ohio and helped rejuvenate his flagging campaign for reelection. It was a clear indication of how divided the country had become during Nixon's presidency.

Nixon's more aggressive approach to the war in Vietnam was somewhat discredited in 1970 when news leaked out that the Army had been covering up massacres of Vietnamese civilians. It was learned that the military had successfully hushed up a U.S. Army massacre of 504 Vietnamese women, children, and old men in a village called My Lai. The massacre had taken place in the spring of 1968 and had been systematically covered up by the Army brass at all levels of command. Later interviews with some of the soldiers present at the massacre said they had been under orders to kill everybody in the village as part of a new "search and destroy" approach to the war. They said the mission was not an unusual one and that such things had been going on for some time. They said that at My Lai, in addition to the murders, rapes and torturing had taken place, and that there had been some mutilation of the civilian's bodies in revenge for American soldiers that had been killed or wounded over the preceding months.

Although the details of the mission were well known (several officers where on the ground during the massacre, and Colonel Oran K. Henderson, the brigade commander who had ordered the attack, observed it all from a helicopter hovering over the village), no action had been taken against the soldiers involved. On the contrary, everyone involved had been told to keep quiet about it.

Two and a years later, in November of 1970, a military trial brought criminal charges against 26 US soldiers who had been involved in the My Lai massacre. By the time the trial was over, all of the charges had been dropped. Only one officer, Second Lieutenant William Calley, a platoon leader, was found guilty. He was convicted of the premeditated murder of 22 Vietnamese civilians, even though he said he was only following direct orders that had been given to him by his superiors.

He was given a life sentence, but the next day, President Richard Nixon canceled the sentence and ordered Calley to be held under house arrest at Fort Benning.

While today we might think that the news that soldiers in Vietnam had been torturing, raping, and killing Vietnamese women and children would lead to public outrage, many rallied to the defense of the soldiers who had participated in the massacre. It was an indication of how divided the country was at that time. Some people were upset to learn there was an Army policy to cover up such occurrences, but at that time, it didn't seem to damage either the Army's credibility or Nixon's. approach to the war. Indiana's governor asked that all state flags to be flown at half-staff in support of Calley and his men. The governors of Utah and Mississippi came out publicly in support of Calley, and against his sentencing. The state legislatures of Arkansas, Kansas, Texas, New Jersey, and South Carolina voted to request clemency for Calley. Alabama's governor George Wallace visited Calley to express his support, and he formally requested that Nixon pardon Calley.

Calley stayed in his personal quarters at For Benning for three and a half years until President Nixon quietly arranged a pardon for him.

The Presidential Election of 1972

In 1972, it was clear that once again, the election was going to take place while the war in Vietnam dragged on.

In the Republican primaries, Nixon's only serious competition came from Congressman Pete McCloskey of California who ran as an antiwar candidate. At the Republican national convention presidential nominating convention, Nixon won easily.

The Democratic race was wide open with fifteen men and two women declaring their candidacy. They were (in alphabetical order):

Shirley Chisholm, U.S. Representative from New York.
Walter Fauntroy, U.S. Representative from Washington, D.C.
Fred Harris, U.S. Senator from Oklahoma.
Vance Hartke, U.S. Senator from Indiana
Hubert Humphrey, U.S. Senator from Minnesota, former VP.
Henry M. Jackson, U.S. Senator from Washington.
John Lindsay, Mayor of New York City, New York
Eugene J. McCarthy, former U.S. Senator from Minnesota
George McGovern, U.S. Senator from South Dakota
Wilbur Mills, U.S. Representative from Arkansa
Patsy Mink, U.S. representative from Hawaii
Edmund Muskie, U.S. Senator from Maine
Terry Sanford, former governor of North Carolina
George Wallace, Governor of Alabama
Sam Yorty, former U.S. Representative from California

The 1972 election also saw the emergence of several third party candidates vying for the presidency. Conservative U.S. Congressman **John G. Schmitz**, a member of the ultra-conservative **John Birch Society**, ran as a representative of the **American Party**, the party that George Wallace had run on in 1968. Schmitz got onto the ballot in 32 states and received 1,099,482 votes, but he won no Electoral College votes.

Linda Jenness was nominated by the **Socialist Workers Party**, with Andrew Pulley as her running-mate.

Benjamin Spock was nominated by the **People's Party**.

1972 was the first time the **Libertarian Party** fielded a candidate. They nominated **John Hospers**, but he was only able to get on the presidential ballot in Colorado and Washington (each state has their own rules about how to get on the presidential ballot, and Colorado and Washington are among the easiest.) Hospers received only 3,573 votes, but he did get one Electoral College vote in Virginia from a **"faithless elector."**

COMMENT:

The term **"faithless elector"** refers to a member of a state's Electoral College who does not vote for the presidential candidate who won the state's popular vote. As stated very specifically in the U.S. Constitution, **members of the Electoral College are not required to vote for the candidate that wins the popular vote**.

It might seem surprising that the framers of the Constitution of this nation *did not even suggest* that members of the Electoral College should vote for the winner of the popular vote. At the time, they wanted the electors to have that freedom in case **the people voted for "the wrong person."** By freeing members of the Electoral College to vote for anyone they chose to, *even if that person was not a candidate*, they assured that political leaders in the states would have the final say about who got to be president.

Faithless electors have never overturned an election, but over the years, there have been many who tried. Below is a brief description of each incident.

In 1796, Samuel Miles, an Federalist elector from Pennsylvania, refused to vote for the winner of the popular vote, Federalist candidate **John Adams**. Instead, he voted for **Thomas Jefferson**, the Democratic-Republican candidate. The Electoral College voting was so close, that had only a few more Federalist electors done the same thing, it would have changed the outcome of the election.

In 1808, six Democratic-Republican electors refused to support **James Madison**, their party's candidate for president, and instead, voted for **George Clinton**, the Democratic-Republican candidate for vie president.

In 1812, three Federalist electors refused to vote for the Federalist vice presidential candidate **Jared Ingersoll**. Instead, they voted for **Elbridge Gerry**, the vice presidential candidate from the opposing Democratic-Republican Party.

In 1820, James Monroe would have received all of the Electoral College votes if **William Plummer, the governor of New Hampshire** and a Democratic-Republican elector hadn't decided at the last minute to cast his vote for his friend, **John Quincy Adams** even though Adams was not a candidate in the 1820 election. Supposedly, Plummer was protesting against the "wasteful extravagance" of the Monroe Administration and used his Electoral College vote to bring attention to the issue. He also voted against **Daniel D. Tompkins**, Monroe's vice presidential choice, saying the man did "not have the weight of character which that office requires."

In 1828, seven of the nine electors from Georgia refused to vote for **Andrew Jackson**'s choice for vice president, **John Calhoun**. Instead, they voted for **William Smith**, a senator from South Carolina who was a vocal opponent of Calhoun. (In 1837, President Andrew Jackson nominated Smith to the Supreme Court, but he declined the honor.)

1832 saw the largest rebellion of electors in history. **Thirty-two electors from Pennsylvania and Maryland** refused to vote for the presidential candidate that had won the popular vote. Two Republican Party electors from Maryland refused to vote for anyone rather than cast their votes for **Henry Clay,** the candidate who had won their state. In Pennsylvania , all 30 electors refused to vote for vice presidential candidate, **Martin Van Buren**, even though he had won the popular vote. Instead, they voted for **William Wilkins**, the senator from their home state of Pennsylvania. Andrew Jackson and Martin Van Buren won anyhow.

1836 saw something happen in the Electoral College that changed the outcome of the 1836 election and could have set a precedent that would change all future presidential elections: some electors refused to vote for the candidate that won the popular vote just because they didn't like his personal behavior. Twenty-three Democratic electors from Virginia refused to cast their votes for the winning Democratic vice president, Richard M. Johnson of Kentucky, because they had learned he was involved in a sexual relationship with an African-American woman. Johnson caused much consternation when he openly admitted he was the father of one of his slave's children. Furthermore, after that slave woman died, he took up sexual relationships with other female slaves, and he was not afraid to tell everybody about it.

With the loss of those 23 votes, there was no majority in the Electoral College, and as specified in the U.S. Constitution, the decision about who would be vice president was sent to the U.S. Senate. In the Senate, with little debate, the senators voted strictly along party lines to name Johnson vice president.

An unusual situation occurred in **1872. Sixty-three of the sixty-six Democratic electors** who were from states Horace Greeley had won voted for somebody else because Greeley had died between the time the election was held and when the Electoral College met. This was something the founding father hadn't considered when they created the Electoral College system. Seventeen of the Greeley electors chose to cast no vote at all, but the other 46 electors voted for whoever they liked personally. They voted for four different candidates for president, and eight different candidates for vice president. However, three of the electors followed what they saw as their duty and voted for the dead man. These votes were later disallowed by Congress, but it is not clear under what authority they disallowed the votes for Greeley because there is no provision in the Electoral College section of the Constitution specifying how such a situation should be dealt with.

As described earlier, the **presidential election of 1876** was the only election in which **Samuel J. Tilden, the candidate that won both the popular vote and the Electoral College vote did not get to be president**. A special Congressional commission, created after considerable contention, voted strictly along party lines to **invalidate many of the Electoral College votes from the South** due to perceived voter fraud. The commission declared the Republican, Rutherford B. Hayes, the Electoral College winner by one vote. Again, it is not clear under what authority they disallowed the Electoral College votes for Tilden. The Electoral College section of the Constitution does not mention any possible circumstance in which the winner of the Electoral College vote can be denied the presidency.

In 1896, four electors, unhappy with their winning vice presidential candidate, Thomas E. Watson, switched their votes to a different vice presidential candidate, Arthur Sewall from Maine.

In 1948, Preston Parks, a Southern Democratic elector from Tennessee, refused to cast his vote for the Democratic winner, Harry S. Truman. Instead, he cast his vote for Strom Thurmond, the segregationist States' Rights candidate. It was a remarkable moment in Electoral College history because it showed that an elector could go so far as to vote for *the opponent* of the winner of the popular vote if the elector had a personal disagreement with the policies of the winner. Strom Thurmond ended up getting 39 Electoral College votes, all from Southern electors.

In 1956, a Southern Democratic elector, **W.F. Turner from Alabama**, voted for his friend, Walter Burgwyn Jones, a U.S. congressman from Alabama (who was not a candidate of any party). The elector didn't like Adlai Stevenson, the winner of the popular vote in Alabama, so he refused to vote for him.

In 1960, one elector planned a revolt that showed the danger of letting a few selected individuals decide who the nation's president would be. **Republican elector, Henry D. Irwin,** from Oklahoma, refused to vote for Richard Nixon, the candidate that had won his state. He simply said he "could not stomach" Nixon. But he went further, he tried to get all the other electors to reject both Nixon and Kennedy and vote instead for two of the most conservative members of the Senate, **Harry Byrd** of Virginia and **Barry Goldwater** of Arizona. He secretly tried to arrange a revolt among the Southern electors, but in the end, the other electors were not willing to go along with his plan (fourteen *unpledged* electors from Mississippi and Alabama *did* cast their presidential votes for Harry Byrd). Although Irwin's plan failed, it did show what could happen if enough of the Electoral College members decided to get together and elect their own preferred candidate. If that happened, according to the wording of the Electoral College section of the Constitution, **there is nothing anyone could do about it.**

In **1968, Republican elector Dr. Lloyd W. Bailey of North Carolina** refused to vote for Richard Nixon (because he had appointed Henry Kissinger) and instead voted for George Wallace. Dr. Bailey pointed out (accurately) that the U.S. Constitution said nothing about him having to vote for the candidate who won his state. He also pointed out (accurately) that George Wallace had won his home district and that before the winner-take-all system had been instituted he would have been obliged to vote for Wallace.

In **1972, Republican elector Roger L. MacBride from Virginia** refused to cast his electoral vote for Richard Nixon, and instead voted for John Hospers, the Libertarian Presidential candidate. He also voted for the Libertarian vice presidential candidate, Toni Nathan, making her the first woman ever to receive an Electoral vote.

In **1976, Republican elector Mike Padden, a lawyer from Washington** refused to vote for the winner of his state, Gerald

Ford, and instead voted for Ronald Reagan (who was not a candidate at that time).

In **1988, Democratic elector Margaret Leach from West Virginia** was shocked when she learned members of the Electoral College were not required to vote for the candidates they were pledged to. She decided to draw attention to this ridiculous situation by switching her votes for president and vice president. She cast her vote for Bentsen for president and Dukakis for vice president and she tried to get the other electors to do the same in order to show the citizens of the United States what was possible with the nonsensical Electoral College system in place. But she was unable to convince any of the others to do what she had done.

In **2000, Democratic elector Barbara Lett-Simmons from the District of Columbia** refused to cast any vote at all. She intended it as a protest against the lack of Congressional representation for the citizens of Washington, DC.

Today, 29 states and the District of Columbia have passed laws that impose penalties on electors who do not cast heir vote for the presidential candidate that wins the popular vote in their state. That means there are **21 states that today still do not even attempt to exert any kind of legal control over how their electors vote**.

So far, it is still not clear if laws that attempt to control how a member of the Electoral College votes are constitutional. Most historians believe the wording of the Electoral College section of the Constitution is no accident; the founding father wanted to be sure the electors *did* have a free rein to vote for anyone they wanted to.

As the 1972 presidential election neared, it was clear that if Nixon was to win reelection, he was going to have to show progress was being made in Vietnam. The public's perception of the war in Vietnam was constantly growing less favorable. They were ready for the war to be over.

As a result, Nixon's campaign message was twofold: first, he tried to convince the American public that the war was going well; second, he had to convince them that his strategy was working to the degree that the war would soon be over, meaning we would be able to get out of the Vietnam mess with some semblance of honor.

Peace talks were still going on in Paris, and just before the election, Henry Kissinger returned to the United States and went before the press to announce that "peace is at hand."

Nixon's message was also positive. He said the U.S. had never lost a war, and "we are not going to lose this one."

Nixon's plan worked. Although the public was fed up with the war in Vietnam, and there were stories being printed in the newspapers about a secret group of "dirty trick's" anti-Democrat operatives that were said to be connected to the White House, Nixon still had plenty of support in the country (the silent majority?). He won the Electoral College vote in every state except Massachusetts.

However, the popular vote was close in some states. For example, Michigan cast 1,961,721 votes for Nixon and 1,459,435 votes for McGovern, and in Wisconsin Nixon only won by 179,256 votes.

When Nixon won the South in 1972, it was **the first time in U.S. history a Republican had won every single Southern state**. After 132 years, it appeared the South had finally forgiven the Republicans for electing Lincoln.

It was clear that with the Republicans finally gaining the upper hand in the South, they would have a much greater chance of winning the presidency in future elections, and that was the way it turned out. Four out of the next five presidents (all except for Ronald Reagan, the very conservative candidate from California), were Southerners. Jimmy Carter was from Georgia, George H. W. Bush was from Texas, Bill Clinton was from Arkansas, and George W. Bush was from Texas.

COMMENT:

The **Paris Peace Accords** were signed in January of 1973. Nixon had ordered intense bombing of civilian areas of North Vietnam in order to force North Vietnam to the peace table, but a much more important concession was that America was ready to leave Vietnam to the Vietnamese. The country would remain divided. The U.S. would train and equip the South Vietnamese Army, but the U.S. military would leave the country.

Although the peace accords ended America's involvement in the war, it didn't end the war. Nixon ordered a "Vietnamization" of the war, a program of training and equipping the Army of the Republic of Viet Nam (ARVN) to be sure they could hold South Vietnam without the presence of U.S. troops.

The Vietnamization program was a complete failure. When the North Vietnamese again invaded the south, the South Vietnamese military was unable to hold them back.

President Nixon had said publicly that if the North Vietnamese invaded South Vietnam again, the United States would again intervene. But when his Secretary of Defense, James R. Schlesinger, stated that he was ready to recommend resumption of the U.S. bombing of North Vietnam, the U.S. Senate quickly passed the **Case-Church Amendment** to prohibit any more direct U.S. involvement in Vietnam.

It could be said that the U.S. role in the Vietnam war began with secret CIA involvement, and ended when the CIA left. Near the end of April, 1975, the last CIA station personnel in Saigon were airlifted off of the roof of the American Embassy by helicopters belonging to Air America , a small airline secretly owned by the CIA.

Chapter Twelve
Secret Presidential Power

As Nixon was winning the presidency in 1972, the American public had just started hearing about a secret security group that was said to be working out of the White House. Soon after the election, more information about the group was beginning to come to light. Known as the **White House plumbers,** the secret group was said to be investigating leaks and other security matters, but when the public found out what the group was really up to, and it would lead to Nixon being the first and only president in U.S. history to be forced to resign the office.

COMMENT:

As the campaigning for the presidential election of 1972 was taking place, members of Nixon's **White House plumbers** group were trying to find out what the Democratic strategy for the election was. On the night of June 17, 1972, they broke into the Democratic National Committee (DNC) headquarters in the **Watergate** building in Washington, D.C. They looked for information about Democratic strategy, and they placed wiretaps in the DNC offices.

A security guard noticed tape on a door that was being used to keep the door from locking. He called the police, and five men, Bernard Barker, Virgilio González, Eugenio Martínez, James McCord, and Frank Sturgis, were caught inside the Democratic National Committee offices and arrested.

As soon as Nixon found out about the arrests, he and his Attorney General John Mitchell began a frantic cover-up to keep the American public from finding out what was really behind the break-in.

Nixon's **presidential Counsel John Dean**, spearheaded the cover-up effort, and at first, Nixon was confident they would be able to distance themselves from it.

But two reporters from the **Washington Post** newspaper, **Bob Woodward and Carl Bernstein**, kept digging and eventually managed to contact an informant who gave them information implicating the president. The two reporters refused to name their informant. They said the informant was known only by the code name, **"Deep Throat"** (many years later the informant was revealed to be Federal Bureau of Investigation Associate Director Mark Felt).

Woodward and Bernstein were able to trace money that had paid to the Watergate burglars. It turned out to be money that had been donated to the president's reelection effort.

Piece by piece, Woodward, Bernstein, and other reporters ferreted out more information about the White House plumbers group. Eventually, all five Watergate burglars were tied directly or indirectly to the Nixon's reelection committee.

On October 10, 1972, a month before the election, Woodward and Bernstein reported that fact in a front page story in the Washington Post. But people either didn't believe the story, or they didn't care. The polls still showed Nixon had plenty of support.

Only one week before the 1972 election, it was revealed that **Attorney General John Mitchell had controlled a secret Republican fund** used to finance intelligence-gathering against the Democrats. Although there were suspicions that Nixon himself was involved, the election results showed the Republicans were still solidly behind him.

Despite intense efforts on the part of the recently reelected president to cover up the whole mess, information continued to come out. Nevertheless, Nixon and other high ranking officials in his administration continued to deny they knew anything about it.

In March of 1973, five months after Nixon had been elected with an overwhelming Electoral College majority, his attorney, John Dean, fearing a prison sentence for himself, began cooperating with the U.S. Attorney's office. He implicated several of Nixon's aides. Nixon continued to deny any knowledge of the plumbers or the cover-up.

In May of 1973, **the U.S. Senate formed a committee to investigate** the whole Watergate affair. The hearings were televised live nationally, and the entire country watched with rapt attention as the story unfolded through the testimony of John Dean and other members of Nixon's inner circle.

One bit of tantalizing information Dean revealed to the committee was that Nixon secretly audio taped all of his meetings. The committee asked Nixon to turn over the tapes, but he refused. It took a series of court battles that eventually led to a decision by the U.S. Supreme Court that he had to comply with the request and turn over transcripts of the tapes. Although forensic analyses of the tapes showed that some conversations had been intentionally erased, they did reveal that Nixon was aware of hush payment to some of the Watergate defendants. The tapes also revealed that Nixon tried to get the CIA to claim that the Watergate break-in was part of a national security investigation.

In July, the House filed **articles of impeachment against Nixon,** citing three articles: 1) obstruction of justice, 2) abuse of power, and 3) contempt of Congress.

At first, some Congressional Republicans stood firm in their support of Nixon, but when more tapes came to light showing how actively Nixon was involved in the cover-up, they too indicated they would be forced to vote for impeachment.

When Nixon heard that even the Republicans in Congress were abandoning him, he went on TV to announce he was resigning the presidency. He left the White House the next day. He was **the first any only U.S. President ever to resign the office**.

Vice President Gerald Ford succeeded him and soon **granted Nixon a full pardon for any crimes he might have committed while president.**

Although with a presidential pardon in hand, Nixon himself could not be prosecuted, a total of 25 officials from the Nixon administration, **including four cabinet members**, were eventually convicted and imprisoned.

The Presidential Election of 1976

After Nixon resigned, **Gerald Ford** served out the remainder of the presidential term and ran for reelection in **1976**.

More and more people were aspiring to be president. In 1976, Fifteen candidates competed in the Democratic primaries, including governors, senators, U.S. representatives, an ambassador, and a housewife. They were (in alphabetical order):

> Robert Byrd, U.S. senator from West Virginia
> Birch Bayh, U.S. senator from Indiana
> Lloyd Bentsen, U.S. senator from Texas
> Jerry Brown, governor of California
> Jimmy Carter, former governor of Georgia
> Frank Church, U.S. senator from Idaho
> Walter Fauntroy, U.S. representative from Washington, D.C.
> Fred R. Harris, former U.S. senator from Oklahoma
> Henry M. Jackson, U.S. senator from Washington
> Ellen McCormack, a housewife from New York
> Terry Sanford, former governor of North Carolina
> Milton Shapp, governor of Pennsylvania
> Sargent Shriver, former U.S. ambassador to France from
>   Maryland
> Morris Udall, U.S. representative from Arizona
> George Wallace, governor of Alabama

As the 1976 primaries went on, it became clear that **Jimmy Carter**, the former governor of Georgia was going to prevail. He was nominated at the Democratic nominating convention and went on to mount an effective campaign as an outsider who would go to Washington to change the kind of politics Nixon had been engaged in.

In the 1976 general election, Carter and his running mate, Walter Mondale from Minnesota, won all the Southern states except Virginia (where they lost by only 22,658 votes).

Ford won most of the Midwestern and Western states, but his controversial pardon of Nixon hurt him the East.

The popular vote was fairly close with 40,831,881 votes going to Carter and 39,148,634 votes to Ford. The Electoral College vote was 297 for Carter and 240 for Ford.

Eugene McCarthy, a former Democratic senator from Minnesota known for his anti-Vietnam position ran as an independent and got 756,631 popular votes, but he didn't win any electoral votes.

The Presidential Election of 1980

As the 1980 presidential election season began, the American people were dismayed over the slow economy, and they were upset about the taking of American hostages in Iran, an incident that became known as the **Iran Hostage Crisis**.

Many were also upset with Carter's decision not to allow U.S. athletes to compete in the 1980 Olympics in Moscow. It was his way of protesting the Soviet invasion of Afghanistan, but many felt the international Olympic movement was a venue to honor the world's best athletes and not a place for political statements. They felt if President Carter's Olympic boycott was allowed to stand, other countries would retaliate and every Olympics would be marred by political posturing.

President **Jimmy Carter** led in most of the Democratic primaries, but **Senator Edward M. (Ted) Kennedy** of Massachusetts was making a strong showing.

By the time the Democratic national presidential nominating convention came around, Carter had enough votes to win, but a strong anti-Carter mood on the convention floor resulted in a last minute "draft Muskie" movement to replace Carter with Secretary of State **Edmund Muskie** from Maine. It failed and Carter was nominated.

COMMENT:

The **Iranian Hostage Crisis** came about in the fall of 1979 after a group of Islamist students and militant revolutionaries took over the American embassy in Tehran.

The revolutionaries were involved in a power struggle with Mohammad Rezā Shāh Pahlavī, **the Shah of Iran** who was supported by the United States as part of **the cold war** with Russia. With the support of Revolutionary leader Ayatollah Ruhollah Khomeini, the militants captured American citizens who had been in the embassy and held them as hostages.

As the months went by, President Carter came under increasing criticism for not doing something about it. Finally, Carter approved a rescue mission code named **Operation Eagle**. The plan was to use helicopters and U.S. Army Delta Force troops to fly into Iran and rescue the hostages, but some of the helicopters suffered mechanical problems and the mission was called off. Unfortunately, as one of the helicopters was being refueled, it collided with the refueling tanker aircraft. The helicopter crashed and soldiers were killed.

More than a year passed before the new government of Iran, now under the control of Ayatollah Ruhollah Khomeini, agreed to release the hostages if the U.S. would agree to release several billion dollars of Iranian assets that had been frozen in American banks when the hostages were first taken. President Carter was secretly working with various international banks to make the deal come about, but it took so long to finalize the details that by the time the hostages were flown out of Iran, Carter had already been defeated by Ronald Reagan. It was the new president that welcomed the hostages home.

The early 1980 Republican primaries indicated that their nominee would likely be former California Governor Ronald Reagan. Reagan was fairly well known outside of California because before being elected governor, he had been a movie actor and had also appeared in many TV commercials.

Baring any unexpected developments, Reagan was sure to win the Republican nomination at the Republican nominating convention. Nevertheless, there were eight others who opposed him They were (in alphabetical order):

John B. Anderson, U.S. Representative from Illinois

Howard Baker, U.S. senator from Tennessee

George H. W. Bush of Texas, U.S. representative and former CIA
    director

John Connally, former governor of Texas

Phil Crane, U.S. representative from Illinois

Bob Dole, U.S. senator from Kansas

Harold Stassen, former governor of Minnesota

Lowell Weicker, U.S. senator from Connecticut

Reagan won the nomination and selected one of his opponents, **George H. W. Bush** of Texas as his running mate.

In the general election, Reagan based his campaign on "**conservative values**," giving Carter ammunition for his accusations that Reagan was a dangerous right wing radical who would take the country down the wrong path.

Although Ronald Reagan had previously been a registered Democrat who supported Roosevelt's very liberal "**New Deal**" policies, his two terms in office as California's Republican governor established his credentials as a **conservative**. His tenure as California's governor took place during a time of **great dissonance in the state over the Vietnam War**. California was a fairly liberal state, but Reagan soon showed that he was going to support the conservative side on most issues. He had plenty of liberal opposition in the state due to his defense of the Vietnam War and his frequent **sarcastic attacks on student antiwar protesters** (he called them "welfare bums").

In the middle of his term as governor, there was a recall effort mounted against him. The recall effort failed which Reagan took as a sign that his policies had the support of the people.

When the anti-Vietnam protests began to grow at California state universities, Reagan frequently used state police to crack down on the protesters. When a large "**people's protest**" was staged at the

University of California campus in Berkeley, he called in state National Guard troops. They occupied the area of the city around the campus for two weeks. When one student, James Rector, was killed by police gunfire, Reagan's response was, "If it takes a bloodbath, let's get it over with. No more appeasement."

Another hotly debated national issue that arose during Reagan's term as governor was the national debate about the legalization of abortion. The liberal State Legislature passed a bill legalizing abortion in California and sent it to Reagan for his signature. After many days of indecision, he signed it (later, during his run for the presidency, he would say he regretted signing it).

The election of 1980 was not even close. Although Carter was a Southerner, the South was now firmly in the Republican camp. Reagan won every Southern state except Alabama (where he lost by only 17,462 votes) and most of the rest of the nation.

Carter even lost his home state of Arkansas, although by only 5,123 votes.

Reagan's Electoral College win of 489-49 was the largest in U.S. history for a candidate running against an incumbent.

Republican Congressman John B. Anderson of Illinois also managed to get himself on the ballot in many states, running as an independent. However, Carter refused to participate in debates with him. When Reagan and Anderson debated, most observers felt Anderson had done very well against the polished actor, Reagan. In the general election, Anderson got 5,719,850 votes but won no electoral votes.

The Presidential Election of 1984

In the presidential election of 1984, Reagan ran for reelection, but being **the oldest president in U.S. history**, there were questions about whether he should be elected for another term. Nevertheless, he dominated the primaries and easily won the nomination at the Republican presidential nominating convention.

After Senator Ted Kennedy again declined to run for president, the Democratic primaries indicated the nomination would come down to three candidates, former vice president, **Walter Mondale** of

Minnesota, Senator **Gary Hart** of Colorado, and civil rights leader **Jesse Jackson** of Illinois.

At the Democratic nominating convention, Mondale won and chose New York Congresswoman Geraldine Ferraro as his running mate. It was the first time a woman had been on the ticket of any major political party. The Democrats hoped she would attract the women's vote.

Mondale and Ferraro immediately began an attack on Reagan's so-called conservative values, saying they were intended to use the threat of communism to scare Americans into going along with extreme government policy. They also said his so-called anti-socialist economic policies were being used to turn Americans against the poor and minorities.

The Reagan campaign focused mostly on his "cold war" foreign policy and on his approach to American economics that had became known as "**Reaganomics**." Reaganomics was the idea that if you get rid of business regulations and cut taxes on the rich, the resulting benefits to the most wealthy would "trickle down" to the middle class.

During the primaries, Reagan had little opposition, although another Republican candidate, George H. W. Bush, derided Reaganomics as "**voodoo economics**."

After the nominations, the nation tuned in to the televised debates. After the first debate, which was limited to domestic policy, most observers felt Reagan had done poorly against Mondale. Reagan seemed hesitant and at times confused. But in the second debate, which was about international policy and national defense, Reagan seemed much more confident.

Even as the debates were going on, the Reagan campaign was producing slick television ads that emphasized the threat from Russia and fostered a "peace through strength" approach to foreign policy. The ads said it was the only way to stop the spread of worldwide communism. These ads drew attention to how much Reagan had strengthened the U.S military during his first term.

COMMENT:

Reagan's cold war foreign policy of fighting communism on all fronts was quite vividly demonstrated in 1983 when a military coup in Granada, a small island off the coast of Venezuela, replaced the government with one that was sympathetic to communist ideals. Reagan immediately sent in 7,000 troops consisting of ranger battalions and airborne paratroopers to depose the new Granada government.

Although most Americans supported the invasion as a necessary part of the fight against communism, it was criticized by the United Kingdom, Canada and the United Nations General Assembly as "a flagrant violation of international law."

Reagan's campaign approach, plus his personal appeal, worked. He won the 1984 general and Electoral College elections easily. He even won 55 percent of the women's vote in the general election **despite the presence of a woman on the Democratic ticket**.

The Mondale-Ferraro ticket won only Mondale's home state of Minnesota and the District of Columbia.

Reagan was a popular president, but information began to leak out that he had created a special task force not unlike the one that had resulted in Nixon's resignation. Further investigation led to what is now known as the **Iran-Contra scandal** (sometimes referred to as **"Irangate"**). The question was, would it hurt Reagan's chances for reelection?

COMMENT:

The **Iran-Contra scandal** began when President Reagan created a secret organization known as "the Enterprise." It was originally created as a way to deal with Iran in order to gain the release of hostages being held by terrorists in Lebanon.

The Enterprise group worked out a deal with the Iranian Army wherein the U.S. would sell weapons to Iran to help with their ongoing war with Iraq, and in return, they would try to secure the release of the hostages.

National Security Adviser Robert McFarlane told President Reagan about the potential deal, but they were stymied because there was an embargo against selling arms to Iran. Reagan wanted to go ahead with the deal anyhow. **Secretary of Defense Caspar Weinberger** and **Secretary of State George Shultz** opposed the deal, but McFarlane and **CIA director William Casey** supported it. With the backing of President Reagan, the plan was put into action.

The result was that arms, including thousands of missiles were sent to Iran, and in exchange,

a few hostages were released, only to be replaced with new hostages. It appeared that Iran had discovered a way to get military arms from the U.S. -- just take hostages and then trade them for weapons.

When the Lebanese newspaper, **Al-Shiraa**, printed an exposé of the deal in November of 1986, President Reagan went on TV to vehemently deny any such deal had been made.

A week later, he admitted the operation *had* occurred, but said it was definitely not an arms-for-hostages deal.

Polls taken at the time indicated most Americans **believed President Reagan was not telling the truth** about the deal. Although Reagan's popularity declined somewhat as more information about the arms for hostages deal, he still had plenty of support among Republicans. They felt that although what he had done might have been illegal, it had been done with good intentions.

That might have been the end of the affair, but it was soon discovered that eighteen million dollars out of the thirty million dollars the Iranians had paid for the American weapons had disappeared. A member of the National Security Council, **Lieutenant Colonel Oliver North**, admitted he had been diverting funds from the arms sales to **the Contras**, a group that was fighting against the communist government in Nicaragua. Although direct support of the Contras was against U.S. law, Reagan was well known as a supporter of the Contras, calling them "the moral equivalent of our Founding Fathers." It was also revealed that

North had been working with drug smugglers and with Panamanian dictator Manuel Noriega to assist the Contras. North said everything he had done had been done **with the full knowledge of National Security Adviser Admiral John Poindexter and, he assumed, with the full knowledge of President Reagan.**

Poindexter resigned and North was fired, but Reagan stated he didn't know anything about it.

To many members of the national media, the connection between the arms sale and the diversion of the money to the Reagan-supported Contra seemed too obvious. They hounded the president about it at every press conference, but Reagan continued to deny any knowledge of what his closest advisors were up to.

Some of Reagan's aides were tried and convicted, but when Reagan's vice president George Bush was elected in 1988, **he pardoned most of them**, including a pardon of Secretary of Defense Caspar W. Weinberger just days before he was to go to trial.

Oliver North was indicted on sixteen felony counts, but they were all later overturned.

Using the publicity he got during the Iran-Contra hearings, North ran for the U.S. senate in 1994 as a Republican against Democrat Charles Robb, son-in-law of President Lyndon B. Johnson. North was able to raise over twenty million dollars to fund his campaign, but he was still defeated.

Since then, North has been a regular commentator on the Fox News Channel and has written several best-selling books.

Chapter Thirteen
Foreign Wars and Presidential Scandal

The Presidential Election of 1988

The presidential election of 1988 saw Vice President **George H. W. Bush** winning **the Republican nomination** by promising to continue the policies of outgoing president Ronald Reagan. He chose Senator **Dan Quayle** from Indiana as his running mate.

With the Iran Contra scandal continuing to unfold, the Democrats were optimistic that they could take back the presidency in 1988. Due to the scandal, they had regained control of the senate after six years of Republican domination.

In 1988, a large number of candidates fought for the Democratic nomination. They were (in alphabetical order):

Douglas Applegate, U.S. Representative from Ohio.
Bruce Babbitt, former Governor of Arizona.
Joe Biden, U.S. Senator from Delaware.
David Duke from Louisiana.
Michael Dukakis, Governor of Massachusetts.
Al Gore, U.S. Senator from Tennessee.
Dick Gephardt, U.S. Representative from Missouri.
Gary Hart, former U.S. Senator from Colorado.
Jesse Jackson from Illinois.
Lyndon LaRouche from Virginia.
Andy Martin from Connecticut.
Paul Simon, U.S. Senator from Illinois.
James Traficant, U.S. Representative from Ohio.

At first, Gary Hart seemed to be the most likely nominee, but questions were raised about his extramarital affairs.

Senator Edward M. Kennedy of Massachusetts again decided against running in 1988, and Arkansas Governor Bill Clinton also declined to run.

Eventually, the convention nominated **Michael Dukakis**, the governor of Massachusetts. He chose U.S. Senator **Lloyd Bentsen** as his running mate.

The 1988 campaign was one of finger pointing. Bush said Dukakis was too liberal, and Dukakis said Bush was too conservative and too militaristic.

Dukakis tried to tie Bush to the Iran-Contra scandal, saying Bush's involvement in the sale of arms to Iran showed Bush had "failed the test of leadership."

In the general election, Bush won the popular vote by about seven million votes (out of ninety million votes cast). In the Electoral College vote, the margin was larger, 426 to 111.

The Republican candidate, Bush, won the South, as was becoming the trend, but he also won California and most of the Midwestern and Northern states. Those were states that the Democrats had counted on winning. (It was the last election in which the Republican candidate won California).

Libertarian Ron Paul from Texas and his running mate, **Andre V. Marrou** from Alaska were also on the ballot in many states. They gathered 431,750 votes nationwide, but no electoral votes.

At first, Bush was a popular president. But a 1990 jump in the price of oil tied to a brief war in **the Middle East** (now known as the **first Gulf War**), a weak economy, and **huge government budget deficits** hurt his popularity.

As the 1992 presidential elections approached, his chances of being reelected seemed in doubt.

COMMENT:

The **first Gulf War** was a military action waged by a UN-authorized coalition of forces against Iraq in response to Iraq's invasion of Kuwait.

In August of 1990, Iraqi troops invaded Kuwait with the intention of annexing the country. It was met by widespread condemnation and immediate economic sanctions against Iraq by some UN member nations.

President Bush sent American ships to the area and **deployed forces in Saudi Arabia** to gather near the Kuwait border. President Bush asked other countries to do the same. Military forces from Saudi Arabia, Britain, and Egypt responded and promised financial support.

Starting **in January of 1991, the U.S. began an aerial bombardment** on Iraqi positions, and much of the aerial attack was shown on American television.

Ground troops soon followed, and within a few days, the Iraqi forces had been pushed back into their own country. As the U.S. ground forces pushed into Iraq, the Iraqi military retreated. At that point, President Bush ordered a cease fire. The war had lasted only a few days, and some in the U.S. criticized the president for not continuing the war. However, both Bush and his Secretary of Defense, Dick Cheney, pointed out that they did not have a UN mandate to do more than push the Iraqis out of Kuwait. They felt further action would have made enemies of their allies in the area.

By the end of hostilities, it is estimated there were between 20,000 and 35,000 Iraq military fatalities plus many thousands of civilian deaths (one estimate put the number of civilian deaths as high as 100,000).

According to the U.S. Department of Defense, U.S. forces suffered 148 battle-related deaths, 35 of them from so-called "friendly fire" (killed by their own troops), and another 145 deaths in non-combat accidents.

The United Kingdom reported 47 deaths, 9 to friendly fire.

Other countries that were involved reported 37 deaths.

The Presidential Election of 1992

The presidential election of 1992 once again brought a third-party candidate to the fore.

President George H. W. Bush ran for reelection and was nominated by the **Republicans**. Although there was some discussion about replacing Dan Quayle as the vice presidential candidate, Bush again chose Quayle.

After a long and contentions primary season, the **Democrats** finally nominated popular Arkansas Governor Bill Clinton over Governor Jerry Brown of California, Senator Tom Harkin of Iowa, Senator Bob Kerrey of Nebraska, former Senator Eugene McCarthy, former Senator Paul Tsongas of Massachusetts, and Governor Douglas Wilder of Virginia.

Clinton chose Tennessee Senator Al Gore to be his running mate.

The surprise of 1992 was the candidacy of Texas billionaire Ross Perot. At one point during the campaign, **he was leading both Bush and Clinton in the national polls**. It seemed as if the public was ready to consider an outsider for president.

The Bush campaign chose a personal attack strategy. They accused Clinton of marital infidelity and draft dodging.

The **Clinton campaign** focused almost entirely on the economy and the fact that the Republicans had a long history of increasing the size of government and thereby increasing the national debt.

Political polling was getting ever more sophisticated, and the polls were indicating that Bush's personal attack strategy wasn't working. People were more concerned with their own pocketbooks.

Another problem for the Republicans was that the cold war was finally cooling down. After a political moderate, Mikhail Gorbachev, was named the General Secretary of the Communist Party of the Soviet Union in 1985, much of the Republican rhetoric about **the worldwide communist threat** fell on deaf ears. By 1989, the Berlin Wall had come down and the phrase "Iron Curtain" was relegated to history. With no looming enemy abroad, all Bush had left to campaign on was his record, and many observers felt Bush's famous 1988 campaign promise of "Read my lips: no new taxes" hurt him in the 1992 election because he had in fact been forced to raise taxes as part of a compromise with Congress.

Midway through the 1992 race, Clinton was still leading in the polls, but when the presidential debates began, Ross Perot made some gains by attacking *both* Bush and Clinton.

Some felt Perot would pull votes away from Clinton, improving Bush's chances for reelection, but Perot was also talking about the poor economy and pointing out how much the Republicans were running up the national debt.

In the end, Clinton's message about the Republican's handling of the economy won out. Clinton won the popular election by 5,805,256 votes (out of 104,423,923 votes cast), but won the Electoral College vote even more convincingly, 370 to 168.

Perot managed to get 19,743,821 votes, but he wasn't able to win a single state and therefore didn't get any Electoral College votes. It seems Perot pulled votes away from *both* Clinton and Bush.

The Presidential Election of 1996

By the time the election of 1996 rolled around, Clinton was being credited with improving the economy, and he was reducing the national debt. He was also successful at keeping the U.S. out of any foreign wars. The absence of a Russian threat, meant he was able to cut some military expenditures which helped reduce the national debt even more.

As soon as President **Clinton announced that he would seek reelection in 1992**, the Republican began to attack his character. They began to criticize his "liberalism" even before they had selected a candidate.

No less than ten serious candidates **fought for the Republican presidential nomination** during the Republican primaries. They were (in alphabetical order):

> Lamar Alexander, former governor of Tennessee.
> Pat Buchanan from Virginia.
> Bob Dole, U.S. Senator from Kansas.
> Bob Dornan, U.S. Representative from California.
> Steve Forbes, a wealthy publisher from New York.
> Phil Gramm, U.S. Senator from Texas.
> Alan Keyes, a former ambassador from Maryland.
> Richard Lugar, U.S. Senator from Indiana.
> Arlen Specter, U.S. Senator from Pennsylvania.
> Pete Wilson, Governor of California.

Pat Buchanan, a well-known conservative, won some of the early Republican primaries, but eventually **Bob Dole** pulled ahead and was nominated as the Republican's 1992 presidential candidate. He chose **Jack Kemp**, a former congressman (and former professional football player) as his running mate.

As the campaign began, Ross Perot once again jumped into the race.

With no serious competition for the Democratic nomination, Clinton was able to get his campaign started early. Without meaningful primary opposition, he was able to focus on the general election early. He raised huge amounts of money and used it to mount a intensive TV campaign.

In order to secure the Republican nomination, Dole had to appeal to the more conservative elements of the Republican party, especially in the South. That gave Clinton the ammunition he needed to paint Dole as a right-winger who would cut popular social programs like Medicare and Social Security.

The relatively young and talkative Clinton came off well in the election debates. In contrast, Dole seemed much older and more hesitant.

Ross Perot's chances of winning any Electoral College votes were dashed when he was left out of the televised presidential debates. (He later sued, claiming an unfair lack of coverage by the TV networks, but his lawsuit was thrown out of court.)

In the 1996 general election, Clinton lost most of the South and the Midwest, but he was able to regain Democratic dominance in California and in the East. He won the popular vote by 8,201,370 votes and won the Electoral College vote 379 to 159.

In his second term, Clinton continued his policy of budget reductions and reduced military expenditures, but in 1998, there was talk on the internet that he was involved in a sexual relationship with a 22-year-old White House intern named Monica Lewinsky. At first Clinton denied the affair, but eventually admitted he had engaged in some sexual "fooling around" with Lewinsky.

The Republicans, who were in control of the House of Representatives at that time, impeached him for trying to cover up the affair.

Although a few past presidents have been threatened with impeachment, President Clinton was only the second president in the history of the United States to **actually be impeached** by the House of Representatives.

COMMENT:

The **Lewinsky scandal**, sometimes referred to as "**Monicagate**," came to light in the fall of 1997 when White House intern, **Monica Lewinsky**, confided to a coworker named **Linda Tripp** that she had been having a sexual affair with President Clinton.

Tripp reported it to **literary agent, Lucianne Goldberg**, who advised Tripp to engage Lewinsky in more conversations about it and secretly record whatever Lewinsky said.

When Tripp did that, Goldberg urged Tripp to take the tapes to **Kenneth Starr**. Starr had been appointed by President Reagan to a federal judgeship, but was at that time a private practice lawyer acting as an independent counsel to investigate some of President Clinton's past real estate investments.

Goldberg began speaking to reporters about the existence of the tapes, and in January of 1998, the Washington Post reported the accusations.

Clinton immediately denied having "sexual relations" with Miss Lewinsky.

His wife, Hillary Clinton, stood by her husband throughout the scandal, describing it as "a vast right-wing conspiracy that has been conspiring against my husband."

By the summer of that year, Lewinsky had been called before a grand jury and had received transactional immunity in exchange for her testimony. She told the grand jury about the affair, and later turned over a semen-stained dress to Starr as DNA evidence proving she was telling the truth.

When Clinton was called before the grand jury, he admitted he had had an "improper physical relationship" with Lewinsky that was "not appropriate." But he defended himself against the charge that he had lied about the affair when he said he had not had sexual relations with her by saying he had not understood that letting her perform oral sex on him could be included in the strict definition of "sexual relations." He said he had never been "the actor," in the affair and had never made physical contact with Lewinsky's "genitalia, anus, groin, breast, inner thigh, or buttocks."

That argument didn't carry much weight with the Republicans in the House of Representatives. They were in the majority and they initiated impeachment proceedings against him. Almost all of the Republicans in the House voted for the majority of the articles of impeachment, and four Democratic representatives from the South voted with them, as did Representative Paul McHale of Pennsylvania.

If a president is impeached by the House of Representatives it is sort of like being indicted for a crime; the "trial," if you want to think of it like that, takes place in the senate. It requires a two-thirds majority of the senators to remove a president from office.

After the senate "trial," 45 Republican senators voted guilty on the charge of perjury, and 55 senators (all of the Democrats and 10 of the Republicans) voted not guilty.

On the charge of obstruction of justice, 50 Republicans voted guilty; 45 Democrats and five Republicans voted not guilty. The vote did not meet the two-thirds majority requirement, so President Clinton was acquitted of all charges and was able to serve out the remainder of his second term in office.

Chapter Fourteen
The Electoral College System Fails Again

The Presidential Election of 2000

Now we come to the all important presidential election of 2000. I hope in the preceding pages I have clarified the complex and often unwieldy way presidents are elected in the United States. With that understanding in mind, let's examine closely the 2000 presidential election in order to understand how a candidate could win the popular vote by 543,895 votes and yet not get to be president.

After the revelation of President Clinton's sexual exploits in the White House and his impeachment for trying to deny it, many wondered how it would affect the Democratic party in the next election. Everybody knew **it would hurt the Democrats**, but no one knew if it would be enough to overcome the positive effect of the Democrats having been in power **during a time of peace with a good economy**.

Al Gore, Clinton's vice president took the position that the affair was behind us and that it had nothing to do with him. He ran for the nomination and won every single state primary election. He selected **Joseph I. Lieberman**, senator from Connecticut as his running mate. (Lieberman was the first observant Jew to be named on the ticket of any major party, and that fact was to have important ramifications in the election.)

The **Republican primaries** were wide open. There were no fewer than 13 candidates vying for the nomination. They were (in alphabetical order):

Lamar Alexander, former governor of Tennessee.
Gary Bauer, former Undersecretary of Education from Kentucky.
Pat Buchanan from Virginia.

George W. Bush, governor of Texas.

Herman Cain from Nebraska.

Elizabeth Dole, former Secretary of Labor from North Carolina.

Steve Forbes from New Jersey.

Orrin Hatch, U.S. Senator from Utah.

Alan Keyes, former U.S. ambassador from Maryland.

John Kasich, U.S. Representative from Ohio.

John McCain, U.S. Senator from Arizona.

Dan Quayle, former vice president from Indiana.

Robert C. Smith, U.S. Senator from New Hampshire.

In the **Republican presidential primaries**, Arizona Senator John McCain took the early lead by winning the New Hampshire primary, but from then on it was mostly wins for George W. Bush, son of former president George H.W. Bush.

At the Republican presidential nominating convention, Bush won easily. He named Texan Dick Cheney, the CEO of military contractor Halliburton Company as his running mate. Cheney had been Secretary of Defense under Bush's father, George H. W. Bush.

When somebody remembered that the Electoral College section of the U.S. Constitution states that the president and vice president cannot come from the same state, Cheney quickly got a driver's license from Wyoming and put his Texas home up for sale.

A third party candidate, **Ralph Nader**, nominee of the **Green Party**, was on the ballot in many states, and as it turned out, his presence on the ballot in Florida undoubtedly cost Gore the presidency.

The 2000 presidential campaign was mainly a battle of television ads, many of them negative (meaning they attacked the opponent rather than extolling the virtues of the candidate who placed the ad).

The three October debates were also important. In the first televised debate, those present in the auditorium felt Bush had performed very badly. In fact, right after the debate ended, Bush's handlers went on TV to attribute his poor showing to illness, saying he had not had adequate time to prepare for the debate. But when the polls came out the next day, a majority of the television viewing audience said they liked what they saw in George Bush. Many of those polled said he seemed like a "regular guy."

Gore accused Bush and the Republicans of being too "right wing" and too militaristic. There was also a lot of talk about where Bush's campaign funds were coming from.

Gore talked about the tax breaks **the wealthiest one percent** were getting, pointing out that it was **the other 99 percent** that were responsible for the country's current prosperity and the budget surplus, so why should the 99 percent have to pay more in taxes and the rich less.

The Bush campaign focused on the "Clinton-Gore" years in an attempt to tie Gore closely to the now-unpopular Bill Clinton.

Gore tried to distance himself from Clinton personally, but did often make reference to how Clinton had turned the budget deficits of the Republican years into a budget surplus.

Bush responded by saying Gore was using "fuzzy math."

The 2000 Election Outcome

Let's start our analysis of the 2000 election by looking first at the outcome. **Gore won the popular vote by 543,895 votes, but lost in the Electoral College by five votes.** Bush's margin of victory in the Electoral College should have been only four votes, but a faithless elector in Minnesota, a state that Gore won, **refused to cast his vote for Gore** and instead cast it for John Edwards.

The obvious question is, how could a candidate who won the popular vote by almost five and half million votes lose in the Electoral College?

The answer goes all the way back to the **constitutional convention** in 1787 when, as a compromise, the delegates agreed to give every state three Electoral College votes, no matter how small the state. Simply put, in the Electoral College, votes cast in a states with small populations count for more that votes in large population states. That reality was created as part of the Electoral College compromise more than two hundred years ago, and because it is in the U.S. Constitution, it is still true today. It would take a vote in Congress to change the Electoral College section of the Constitution, and then it would require ratification by three-fourths of the states. That is not likely to happen because the states with smaller populations would lose their advantage in selecting the president. Today, because the Republicans generally win the smaller states, they would undoubtedly block any attempt to get rid of the Electoral College system.

2000 presidential Election Results Region by Region.

Gore won the entire West Coast accounting for 7,829,197 of his popular vote total.

Gore also won **the East**, except for New Hampshire which he lost by only 7,211 votes.

In just three of the eastern states he won -- New Jersey, New York, and Pennsylvania -- he got 7,878,047 popular votes. As you can see, Gore racked up large pluralities in the states with the largest populations.

In **the Midwest**, Bush won the all-important Ohio vote with it's 21 Electoral College votes. However, Bush only won the popular vote by 165,019 (out of almost five million votes cast). In other words, in Ohio, Gore got **almost as many** votes as Bush, but got **zero Electoral College votes**.

In the **central Midwest, Gore won** Illinois, Iowa, Michigan, Minnesota, and Wisconsin which gave him 7,809,214 more popular votes.

It is important to note that in the states Gore won, **Nader was also strong**. Some say Gore would have won as many as a million more votes **if Nader had not been on the ballot** in those states, but that wouldn't have resulted in Gore wining **any more** electoral votes. Without Nader in the race in those states, **it is likely Gore would have won the popular vote by one and half million votes, but he still would not have been elected president.** (Those numbers will be important later when we analyze the potential popular votes for Obama in the upcoming 2012 election.)

Bush won Western states with small populations, including Colorado, Idaho, Kansas, Montana, Nebraska, Nevada, North Dakota, Oklahoma, South Dakota, Utah, and Wyoming to accumulate **60 Electoral College votes**. The total number of voters in those states in

2000 was 9,394,171. In comparison, California had 10,965,856 voters, more than a million and a half more voters than the small Western states, and yet **California only got 54 Electoral College votes**. It clearly illustrates the advantage the smaller-population states have in the Electoral College.

Bush won every Southern state, but in some of those states **the vote was close**. The only Southern states Bush won convincingly were Texas, his home state, and Alabama. In the other Southern states, the vote was surprisingly close. In Tennessee, Bush won the popular vote by only 80,229 (out of more than two million votes cast). In Arkansas, he won by only 50,172 votes (out of almost a million votes cast). That meant Bush was picking up **all** the Electoral College votes in the South, but he wasn't gaining much advantage in the popular vote count.

In Florida, the outcome was extremely close, with Bush pulling out a very narrow win of 1,784 votes (out of 6 million votes cast).

However, the state-mandated recount found many irregularities. Somehow, a lot of votes for Gore had been missed. After the recount was finished, Bush's lead had been cut to only 537 votes. A second, more careful recount was ordered, and **the more votes that were recounted, the more Bush's lead dwindled**. When Bush's lead was down to only 154, Republicans went to court to put a stop to the recount. The Florida state Supreme Court said the recount was legal an should go on, but in an extremely controversial decisions, the U.S. Supreme Court, in a 5 to 4 vote, ordered the recount stopped permanently.

With the addition of Florida's 25 electoral votes, **Bush had 271 Electoral College votes, just one more than the required 270 needed to win the election**. Gore ended up with 266 electoral votes (one Gore elector from the District of Columbia left her ballot blank to protest their lack of representation in Congress). **Even though Al Gore had won the general election by more than half a million votes, he did not get to be president**.

It is interesting to note here that the framers of the Constitution intentionally left the members of the Electoral College free to vote for anyone they wanted to, possibly for just such a situation. A few Republican electors could have realized it was unfair that the candidate who won the national vote was losing in the Electoral College and **they could have legally switched their votes to the winner of the popular vote**, Al Gore.

COMMENT:

The **Florida voting outcome in the 2000 presidential election** was very controversial, to say the least. With Bush's conservative Republican brother serving as the governor in Florida, most observers thought Bush would win the state's presidential election easily.

But Clinton had been a popular president there, and the state also had a large Hispanic and African-American population that traditionally voted Democratic. And although the fact that Gore's running mate, Joe Lieberman, was Jewish might have hurt the Democrats in the rest of the South, the large Jewish population in Florida ended up voting mostly for the Gore-Lieberman ticket.

The early pre-election polls showed the race was going to be closer in the state than people thought.

Soon after the polls closed, based on exit polling (the pollsters question voters as they leave the polling places), the national TV networks declared Gore the projected winner in Florida. Based on that result, they also projected Gore would win the Electoral College vote and therefore he would become the nation's forty-third president.

A significant moment in the election came after the TV networks had officially declared Gore their projected winner. Reporters asked if Bush was ready to concede Florida based on the exit poll results. Bush reminded them that his brother was the governor of Florida and went on to say we haven't given up yet, we are "working the phones." When the reporters asked what good "working the phones" would do now that the polls were already closed, there was no answer from either George Bush or his brother. Later that night, more results began to come in favoring Bush.

That kind of thing, along with the many voting irregularities that were being reported in Florida, made the Democrats suspicious. When voting results came in showing Bush had somehow overcome Gore's lead and had won by 1,784 votes, they got even more suspicious.

With a win that close (a Bush advantage of 1,784 votes out of 5,963,110 votes cast), Florida law required an automatic recount.

The closely scrutinized recount found Bush to have won **by only 537 votes.** The recount **had taken 1,247 votes away from Bush.**

The Democrats starting looking for other voting irregularities. They said in Escambia County, a predominately African-American district, 16% of the ballots were thrown out without explanation. In Columbia County, another predominately African-American district, 17% of the ballots were rejected. They analyzed the districts in which the largest numbers of ballots were thrown out and found out it **was happening in Democratic districts.**

The Democrats began to analyze the 54,000 Florida citizens that had not been allowed to vote for one reason or another. Again, the majority of citizens that had not been allowed to vote were African-Americans. Further analysis discovered that many African-American voters had been turned away because **their names had mistakenly been listed as felons.**

One thing that drew special attention from the Democrats was a confusing type of paper ballot used in Palm Beach that became known as the "**butterfly ballot.**" They said the Palm Beach voters were mostly Democrats who had been confused by the ballots which had **made them mistakenly vote for Pat Buchanan of the Reform Party** when they thought they were voting for Al Gore. Buchanan received 3,407 votes on the so-called butterfly ballots, and later, the chairman of the Palm Beach County's Reform Party said he believed there were only 400 to 500 Buchanan supporters in that Democratic stronghold. An analysis of the ballots showed most of those who had voted for Buchanan had otherwise voted Democratic. (Exit polls had previously indicated that most of the voters in that district said they had voted straight Democratic.) Later, Buchanan himself said, after looking at one of the so-called butterfly ballots, he could see how voters might have mistakenly voted for him when they thought they were voting for Al Gore.

For all these reasons, the Gore campaign requested that **disputed ballots in four counties be counted by hand,** Under Florida law, such a recount was allowable.

Although thousands of spoiled Bush-favoring absentee ballots from overseas soldiers **had been** recounted by hand to determine "the **voter's intent,**" the Bush campaign **fought hard against a manual recount of the rest of the votes. Katherine Harris,** the Republican Secretary of State in Florida stopped the recount. That prompted the Democrats to go to court to say that under Florida law, a manual recount should be allowed.

Harris argued against the recount in court until it was finally brought before **the Florida Supreme Court. They ordered the recount to be completed,** and it was resumed.

The problem for Bush was that the more ballots were recounted, the more votes Bush lost. After careful scrutiny of the ballots, Bush's 1,784 vote lead soon shrank to only 154. **It was clear that if the recount was allowed to go on, Bush would lose.**

In desperation, the Republicans **asked the U.S. Supreme Court for an emergency decision to stop the recount.** They said Bush would suffer "irreparable harm" if the recount was allowed to continue.

The court's decision came quickly: **the Supreme Court voted five to four to permanently stop the recount.**

To this day, that decision is still one of the most controversial in the Supreme Court's history. The decision, and more importantly, the close 5-4 vote, is often used as an example when people talk about the president's power to "stack" the Supreme Court. Cynics would say you could have told in advance which of the judges were going to vote to stop the recount by simply noting which president appointed them.

The five judges who voted to stop the recount were:

Anthony Kennedy, appointed by Republican President Ronald Reagan.

Antonin Scalia, appointed by Republican President Ronald Reagan.

Sandra Day O'Connor, appointed by Republican President Ronald Reagan.

William Rehnquist, appointed by Republican President Richard Nixon.

Clarence Thomas, appointed by Republican President George H. W. Bush.

The four judges who voted against stopping the recount, Ruth Bader Ginsburg, Stephen Breyer, David Souter, and John Paul Stevens were quite vocal about their **opposition to the decision**. They denounced the decision as **a violation of both constitutional procedures and democratic principles**. They said the Florida Supreme Court was clearly within its legal and constitutional rights in allowing the recount to go forward, and therefore it was not appropriate for the U.S. Supreme Court to step in and override the highest court in the state of Florida. Justice Stevens pointed to historical legal precedent, saying, "On questions of state law, we have consistently respected the opinions of the highest courts of the states."

As for the strictly legal issues, the four dissenting judges said **the Republicans had failed to provide a legal basis** for the issuance of a stay. They said there was no evidence that Bush would suffer irreparable harm if the recount went on (other than he might lose the election). They asked how, in a democracy, carefully counting every vote could be a bad thing. They said the only danger of "irreparable harm" was to the public and to the democracy, and that going against Florida law to stop a recount would "cast a cloud on the legitimacy of the election."

Four of the five judges that had voted in favor of Bush's request to stop the Florida recount had nothing to say about why they had made that decision. Only Antonin Scalia commented, saying only that the decision had been made because there was no way to know if the ballots that were being counted were "legally cast."

> The dissenters pointed out that there was nothing in the Bush request to stop the recount that said anything about "legally cast ballots." On the contrary, they said, that was exactly the reason for the recount, to make sure very ballot counted had been legally cast.
>
> Nevertheless, the Supreme Court is the final law of the land and the recount was stopped. **Katherine Harris** certified the election in favor of Bush and there was nothing Gore or the Democrats could do abut it.

Perhaps the most surprising outcome of the 2000 presidential election was the lack of outrage by the public over the fact that the winner of the popular votes did not get to be president.

Remember the 1824 election when Andrew Jackson had won the nation's popular vote, but didn't get to be president? Back then, the nation erupted in outrage. They said the people's wishes had been trampled. Many demanded that the election be overturned and that Jackson be put into his rightful place as president.

When that didn't happen, Jackson demanded an end to the Electoral College system of electing the president. He said it was ridiculous that the people didn't get to vote for the most important office in the country. Nearly everyone agreed with him, but of course, the states with smaller populations were not about to give up their voting advantage in the Electoral College, so nothing was done.

So what was different in 2000? Why did Gore, unlike Andrew Jackson, give up so easily?

In 1824, Jackson immediately said he would run again for president in the 1828 election, and he used the unfairness of the 1824 election as his main reason why he should be president. As a result, he won the 1828 election in a landslide.

So why didn't Gore do the same thing that Jackson had done in 1824? Many think that if he had run again and kept on reminding people of what had happened in Florida and of the fact that he had actually won the 2000 election by 543,895 votes, he would have won the 2004 presidential election easily. But that didn't happen. The reasons are complex and unfortunate, as we shall see.

Chapter Fifteen
Presidential Politics and the War on Terrorism

By the time the 2004 presidential election rolled around, Al Gore and the Electoral College debacle of 2000 was long forgotten because the nation was in an uproar over the events that had been put into motion on **September, 11, 2001**. On that date, 19 young men from Egypt, the United Arab Emirates, Lebanon, and Saudi Arabia commandeered four airliners in order to crash them into politically-important American buildings.

COMMENT:

The events of September 11, 2001 were put into play many months before when a few young Arab-looking men who spoke little English but had legal U.S. entry visas, asked about pilot training in San Diego. Through a translator, they said they wanted to learn to fly Boeing passenger jets, but they were told they would have to learn to fly small airplanes first. They said no, they were only interested in learning how to fly big passenger airliners. The flying instructors testified later that they thought the young men had big unrealistic dreams.

After the flying instruction began, the instructors said the students focused only on in-flight maneuvering and had little interest in learning about takeoffs and landings.

Later, other young men from Saudi Arabia entered the U.S. and began taking flying lessons in Florida where they eventually obtained commercial pilot's licenses. They never actually got the chance to fly any large planes, but in the spring of 2011, they were able to get training on a Boeing 737 simulator in Arizona.

That triggered interest from somebody who notified the Arizona FBI. The Arizona branch of the FBI alerted Washington headquarters that several Middle Easterners were training at a U.S. aviation school in Arizona, They recommended that other aviation schools nationwide be contacted to find out if other Arabs might be trying to learn how to fly large airplanes.

It is not known if anybody in the FBI, or in any other antiterrorist agency, took note of the warning. However, the FBI and other agencies must have been aware that airliner hijackings had long been a favorite way for militant groups to bring their causes to the public's attention. Over the previous forty years, there had been several instances where airliner hijackers reported that they were planning to crash their hijacked airliners into important buildings.

It is not known how far up the line the Arizona FBI report went, but it is now known that at least two of the hijackers were already on an FBI watch list.

After completing their pilot training in August of 2001, the hijackers bought tickets on four flights leaving from Eastern cities with destinations in California. Planes leaving for cross-country flights were intentionally chosen to be sure they would have heavy loads of fuel on board.

Using box cutters as weapons and with the threat that bombs on board the plane, the five hijackers took control of American Airlines Flight 11 that had left Boston's Logan Airport at 7:59 AM. The hijackers flew that airliner into the North Tower of the World Trade Center at 8:46 AM.

Another airliner, American Airlines Flight 175, took off from Boston's Logan Airport at 8:14 AM. Five more hijackers took control of that airliner and flew it into the South Tower of the World Trade Center at 9:03 AM.

American Airlines Flight 77 took off from Washington's Dulles International Airport at 8:20 AM and another five hijackers took control of that plane and flew it into the Pentagon Building at 9:37 AM.

A forth airliner, United Airlines Flight 93 took off from Newark International Airport at 8:42 AM, and four more hijackers took control of that plane. Reportedly, several of the passengers tried to overcome the hijackers and the plane crashed into the ground near Shanksville, Pennsylvania at 10:03 AM.

Video of the two World Trade Center towers burning was soon being broadcast live on all the TV networks, and the nation watched in horror.

Unexpectedly, the south tower, the second tower to be hit, collapsed after burning for 56 minutes. Twenty one minutes later, the north tower also collapsed.

Later analysis determined that the collapse of both buildings was caused by the fire, not by the impact. The heat of burning jet fuel had melted important steel structural elements of the buildings. According to the 9/11 commission report, the buildings would not have collapsed if more fireproofing had been installed.

By the end of that dreadful day, 2,606 people had died in the two towers and 125 had died at the Pentagon. On the four airliners, 246 passengers and crew had died, along with the19 hijackers.

The attacks on 9/11 brought about many changes in the United States. In less than a month, U.S. military forces launched attacks in Afghanistan. It was the first stage of President Bush's new "war on terror." He said from now on, U.S. policy would be to go after terrorists and that the U.S. would not distinguish between terrorist organizations and nations or governments that harbored them.

Bush focused on one particular group of terrorists known as **al-Qaeda**, a widespread group of militants led by a Saudi citizen named **Osama bin Laden**. He was believed to be in Afghanistan, and it was believed he was in league with the Taliban, an Islamist militant group that controlled Afghanistan at that time.

As U.S. forces, with support from Britain and Australia, approached Kabul, the capital city of Afghanistan, the Taliban retreated. By the middle of November, the allied forces were in control of the country. (As of this writing, eleven years later, there are still 80,000 U.S. troops and an unknown number of military-support **"private contractors"** in Afghanistan.)

In the spring of 2003, President Bush's war on terror was expanded to Iraq. Alleging that **Iraq was harboring al-Qaeda** and that Iraqi President Saddam Hussein was in the process of developing **weapons of mass destruction,** President Bush sought approval from Congress to invade Iraq. Although Congress did not approve a formal declaration of war against Iraq, they did pass a joint resolution **authorizing military action** against Iraq. It was not an uncontested vote. In the House, the Republicans were nearly unanimously in favor of it, 215 to 6, but the Democrats votes against it, 126 to 82. The dissenters pointed out that United Nations inspectors had done a complete search of Iraq and had found **no evidence of any weapons of mass destruction** development and **no evidence of an al-Qaeda presence**. In fact, the United Nations experts said the brutal government of Iraq had been making sure there was no support for al-Qaeda in the country.

In the Senate, the Republicans, of course, supported their Republican president and voted in favor of military action, 48 to1. But what was surprising was that the majority of the Democratic senators also voted in favor, 29 to 21 against. It was not so surprising that essentially all of the senators from the conservative Southern and middle Western states voted in favor of military action in Iraq, but it was a surprise to many that some senators from the more liberal Northern states also voted in favor of it. Senators like Kerry from Massachusetts, Clinton and Schumer from New York, Biden and Torricelli from New Jersey, Carper from Delaware, Feinstein from California, and Cantwell from Washington voted in favor of taking military action in Iraq.

However, by 2007, 28 of the 77 senators who had voted in favor of military action in Iraq said that if they knew then what they know now, they would have voted against the measure, meaning it would have failed in the senate, and Bush would not have had the authority to send U.S. troops to Iraq.

With congressional approval in hand, President Bush soon ordered air attacks on Iraq, and on March 20, 2003, the military invasion of Iraq began. With the support of extensive air power, the U.S. forces moved quickly, and within a few weeks, they took the capital city of Baghdad.

A month later, speaking from the deck of a U.S. aircraft carrier, USS Abraham Lincoln, President **Bush said the war in Iraq was over** and a new era in Iraq could begin.

In reality, it took more than eight more years and a new president before the last of the U.S. troops were withdrawn from Iraq.

All told, **well over a million members of the U.S. military** served in Iraq.

Despite the best medical care in any U.S. war, **4,484 American soldiers died** in Iraq, many of them from insurgent ambushes and from so-called **"improvised explosive devices"** (IEDs).

317 coalition forces from countries other than the U.S. also died in combat.

Estimates of the numbers of wounded American soldiers **vary widely from 100,000 to more than half a million,** depending on what type of injuries are counted.

The number of deaths and injuries to Iraqi civilians is unknown. **Civilian death estimates vary from 151,000 to over a million.** The number of injuries and deaths of Iraqi civilians **will probably never be known.**

At the end of 2011, President Obama withdrew the last of the U.S. troops from Iraq, but the war in Afghanistan goes on, making it the longest war in U.S. history.

The Presidential Election of 2004

The presidential election of 2004 was obviously going to be a referendum on the war in Iraq. Despite President Bush's pronouncement that the war was over in March of 2003, a year later, no weapons of mass destruction had been found and American soldiers were still dying over there.

There was also widespread criticism of Bush's conduct of the war, especially after accusations of torture, rape, and murder of military prisoners came out. Of special focus was the Abu Ghraib prison in

Iraq and the Guantanamo Bay detention camp in Cuba, both of which were managed by the U.S. military.

Nevertheless, no serious challengers appeared during the Republican primaries, and as a result, Bush was nominated by the Republican party to run for reelection. There were calls for him to dump his vice president, Dick Cheney, because he was such a strong advocate of what he referred to as "enhanced interrogation" of prisoners of war. Bush refused.

The Democratic primaries saw 10 candidates come forward. They were (in alphabetical order):

Wesley Clark, retired U.S. Army general from Arkansas.
Howard Dean, former governor of Vermont.
John Edwards, U.S. Senator from North Carolina.
Dick Gephardt, U.S. Representative from Missouri.
Bob Graham, U.S. Senator from Florida.
John Kerry, U.S. Senator from Massachusetts.
Dennis Kucinich, U.S. Representative from Ohio.
Joe Lieberman, U.S. Senator from Connecticut.
Al Sharpton, civil rights activist from New York.
Carol Moseley Braun, former senator from Illinois.

In the **Democratic primaries**, **Howard Dean** was the early favorite, but **John Kerry** pulled out a win in **New Hampshire**.

Then, in the **South Carolina** primary, **John Edwards** won.

In **Oklahoma**, **Wesley Clark** won, but Edwards was a close second.

But then, Kerry started to win some primaries. He won Hawaii, Idaho, Maine, Michigan, Nevada, Tennessee, Washington, and Washington, D.C. and then went on to win at the Democratic national nominating convention. He selected North Carolina Senator **John Edwards** as his running mate

The 2004 presidential campaign was, as predicted, mostly about Iraq and U.S. foreign policy. Kerry attacked Bush's handling of the war in Iraq, and he especially criticized the treatment of prisoners in Guantanamo Bay without regard to the Geneva Conventions, the body of international law that regulates the treatment of prisoners of war. Kerry said Bush had repeatedly acted without the support of the

United Nations, and his actions were hurting America's reputation abroad, even among America's allies.

Bush's campaign focused on the **worldwide terrorist threat**, and it seemed eerily similar to earlier Republican presidential campaigns during the Cold War that had focused on the **worldwide communist threat**.

During the campaign, Bush defended his aggressive approach to fighting terrorism. One of his early campaign ads showed a picture of an Arab-looking man as it talked about the need to fight terrorism at home and abroad. His ads suggested Kerry would be weak on fighting terrorism. They suggested that in a crisis, Kerry would be slow to act.

The Kerry campaign responded by pointing out that he voluntarily served in Vietnam and had won service metals while Bush was "hiding out" in the Texas National Guard."

The Democrats said that Bush had used his father's political connections in Texas to get into easy Texas National Guard assignment. They said Bush rarely even bothered to perform his National Guard duties. They produced evidence that showed he was actually out of the state when National Guard records showed he was in attendance at National Guard meetings in Texas.

The Republicans tried to discredit the Texas National Guard documents, and they found some Vietnam veterans willing to say that Kerry's "dangerous" service in Vietnam was exaggerated, and that he didn't deserve the medals he had won. They pointed out that upon his return to the United States, Kerry had joined the veterans against the war in Vietnam movement, thus betraying his former comrades.

The Republicans also tried to discredit the reporters who had reported on Bush's missing service in the Texas National Guard.

In every instance, Bush defended his conduct of the "**war on terrorism**." His ads continued to focus on the Arab threat.

The implication was clear, if the voters liked his "preemptive" approach to fighting Arab terrorism in Afghanistan and Iraq, and if they felt the harsh treatment of Arabic prisoners was a fitting response to the Americans who had died on 9/11 and a way to get information that might help the U.S. military, then they should vote to reelect Bush and Cheney.

As it turned out, **Bush and Cheney won every Southern state, and many of the Midwestern and Western states. Kerry won the West Coast, the upper Midwest, and the East.**

While **the popular vote was relatively close,** 50.73 percent to 48.27 percent in favor of Bush, the Electoral College vote was not as close -- 286 for Bush and 251 for Kerry. Once again, the Republican dominance in the South and in the Western states with smaller populations had racked up enough Electoral College votes to win.

The Presidential Election of 2008

The **Presidential Election of 2008** was clearly going to be a referendum on how well Bush and the Republicans had handled the so-called war on terror. By the time the 2008 presidential election season began, national polls were indicating Bush would leave office as **one of the most unpopular presidents in U.S. history**. The polls showed he was even more unpopular than Richard Nixon after Nixon was forced to resign.

It was quite **a contrast to Bush's 90 percent approval rating** when he stood on the deck of the aircraft carrier USS Abraham Lincoln and declared "mission accomplished" in Iraq.

Paradoxically, when asked in 2008 why they disliked Bush's performance in office so much, most people mentioned the same thing that had formerly made him popular, the war in Iraq.

Vice President Dick Cheney's ratings were even lower than Bush's, with only thirteen percent of Americans saying they approved of his performance in office.

Nevertheless, **Bush and Cheney still had plenty of support among Republicans in the South**.

With the polls showing such strong disapproval of Bush, the Republicans undertook the uphill task of getting a Republican elected president in 2008.

Eleven candidates came forward to compete in the Republican primaries. They were (in alphabetical order):

Sam Brownback, U.s. Senator from Kansas.
Jim Gilmore, former Governor of Virginia.

Rudy Giuliani, former mayor of New York City.
Mike Huckabee, former Governor of Arkansas.
Duncan Hunter, U.S. Representative from California.
Alan Keyes, former ambassador from Maryland.
John McCain, U.S. Senator from Arizona.
Mitt Romney, former Governor of Massachusetts.
Tom Tancredo, U.S. Representative from Colorado.
Fred Thompson, former U.S. Senator from Tennessee.
Tommy Thompson, former Governor of Wisconsin.

The **Republican primaries** began, as usual with the Iowa caucuses. Mike Huckabee won, but then faded badly in New Hampshire. McCain won New Hampshire despite speculation that Rudy Giuliani or Mitt Romney would prevail.

After a third-place finish in Florida, Giuliani withdrew from the race and endorsed John McCain. From then on, **McCain** won most of the primaries, and he was nominated at the Republican national nominating convention in Minnesota. He surprised everyone by picking the outspoken conservative governor of Alaska, **Sarah Palin**, as his running mate.

With Bush's approval rating so low and the American public tired of hearing about the continuing deaths of American servicemen in Iraq and Afghanistan, the Democrats felt they had a good chance of taking back the White House in 2008.

Ten candidates came forward to compete in the Democratic primaries. They were (in alphabetical order):

Evan Bayh, U.S. Senator from Indiana.
Joe Biden, U.S. Senator from Delaware.
Hillary Clinton, U.S. Senator from New York.
Christopher Dodd, U.S. Senator from Connecticut.
John Edwards, former U.S. Senator from North Carolina.
Mike Gravel, former U.S. Senator from Alaska.
Dennis Kucinich, U.S. Representative from Ohio.
Barack Obama, U.S. Senator from Illinois.
Bill Richardson, Governor of New Mexico.
Tom Vilsack, former Governor of Iowa.

Many were surprised that Al Gore, the winner of the popular vote in 2000, wasn't among the candidates. At first he expressed interest, but eventually he decided against running again. The speculation was that he felt he was doing more good as an ambassador in **the fight against global warming**.

In the Iowa caucuses, the relatively unknown, but very eloquent, Barack Obama won, with John Edwards coming in second and Hillary Clinton third.

But Clinton made a comeback to win in New Hampshire.

There were January primaries in Michigan and Florida, both won by Clinton, but the Democratic National Committee disallowed them because they were held too early in the primary season. (Eventually, the Michigan and Florida votes were divided between Clinton and Obama.)

At the end of January, Obama won Nevada and South Carolina, but from that point on, Obama and Clinton alternated wins in the rest of the primaries.

The 2008 Democratic national presidential nominating convention was expected to be contentious with the delegates votes split between Obama and Clinton. Neither candidate had enough votes to win the nomination. However, midway through the voting, when it became clear that Obama was pulling into the lead, Clinton asked for Democratic unity and told her delegates to vote for Obama.

Barack Obama, the first-term senator from Illinois, was nominated by unanimous acclamation. He was the first person of African-American heritage to be nominated by a major party (his mother was white, but she had married Kenyan Barack Hussein Obama Sr. while he was in the U.S going to college).

Obama chose **Joe Biden**, a U.S. senator from Delaware, as his running mate.

The campaign focused on the two ongoing wars in Afghanistan and Iraq. Obama came out strongly against the Iraq war in particular, and McCain, who had supported the two wars all along, was forced to defend them.

Focusing on Bush's unpopularity, Obama reminded the voters that McCain had voted to support Bush 90 percent of the time.

McCain, as a long-time member of the U.S. Senate, focused on Obama's inexperience. He pointed out the fact that Obama was **a first-term senator**.

Obama countered that charge by saying it was time for a change. He pointed out how the Republicans had turned Clinton's healthy economy and budget surplus into an unhealthy economy and a rapidly-growing budget deficit. He said he would enact universal health care, make America "green," and bring back respect for America abroad.

COMMENT:

By the time voters went to the polls in 2008, the country was in the midst of a financial crisis. Only a few weeks before the 2008 election, Lehman Brothers, one of the world's largest financial institutions was forced to file for bankruptcy because of its exposure to newly-created risky and speculative financial instruments that were based on shaky subprime mortgages. Many other financial institutions around the world were also highly exposed to the new and very complicated financial instruments.

As the election neared, the situation was threatening to bring down America's entire financial system. Bush's Secretary of the Treasury, Henry Paulson, the former head of the Goldman Sachs investment banking company, had gone before Congress to ask for hundreds of billions to bail out the financial institutions. After much controversy, Congress finally authorized the money, and the crisis was averted for the time being. Nevertheless, investors in the stock market lost billions and the so-called "housing bubble" collapsed and many Americans found they owed much more on their homes than they were worth. With unemployment rising, many faced foreclosure.

As of this writing, with the 2012 presidential election season already underway, unemployment is still high and some parts of the economy are still struggling. The financial crisis of 2008 and the government's handling of it is sure to be one of the most important issues in the 2012 election campaign.

As election day neared in 2008, the polls were showing the economic crisis was by far the most important issue. Although Americans were aware of Obama's inexperience, that seemed to be less important than the fact that people were hurting economically and they wanted a change in Washington.

The election took place in an environment of financial anxiety and uncertainty. Although the Republicans again held most of the South, this time they lost Florida in a very close vote (McCain lost Florida by 236,148 votes out of eight million votes cast).   McCain also lost Virginia in another close vote, and he lost North Carolina, but by only 14,177 votes (out of more than four million votes cast).

Obama won the East, some of the Midwest, and the West Coast. But McCain won 28 states, more than Obama's 22. However, McCain's wins were all in states with smaller populations and fewer Electoral College votes. Obama won all the larger population states *and* enough of the South and Midwest to secure the Electoral College win and become the 44th president of the United States.

Chapter Sixteen
The Upcoming Presidential Election of 2012

Now we come to the presidential election that will take place this year on November 6, 2012.

As of this writing, neither party has nominated a candidate, but it seems clear that the Democrats will nominate Barack Obama for reelection, and the Republicans will nominate former Massachusetts governor, Mitt Romney.

This time, it seems likely the two biggest campaign issues will be war and the economy. President Obama has withdrawn most of the U.S. troops from Iraq, but the situation there is still unstable. What will happen without a U.S. military presence there is an open question. If there is a flare-up of violence in Iraq, it could have a significant impact on the outcome of the 2012 U.S. presidential election.

The war in Afghanistan goes on, even though President Obama has promised a gradual draw down of U.S. troops there.

Due to Obama's decision to pull U.S. troops out of Iraq, Romney may try Bush's approach of **saying the Democrats are weak on the war on terror**. But the effectiveness of that argument might be somewhat diminished by the fact that President Obama ordered the CIA and Navy SEALs operation that went into Pakistan and killed **Osama bin Laden**, the leader of al-Qaeda.

Although the U.S. economy is slowly recovering from the financial crisis, there is still **considerable dissonance** in the country over the way the government handled **the bailouts** and about the perceived unfairness of the various financial stimulus programs that seemed to only help those large financial institutions that had caused the economic crisis in the first place.

The one thing that is clear from the early polls is that the election will be close. It will probably come down to which candidate can hold their party's traditionally strong regions of the country.

It's possible that the last-minute appearance of a viable third-part candidate could complicate things as it did in the presidential election of 2000 when third-part candidate Ralph Nader is believed to have taken enough votes away from Al Gore to cost him the presidency.

At this point, the only way to figure out the likely outcome of the 2012 presidential election is to look at it in terms of the Electoral College, which is, as we have learned, the actual way Americans elect presidents.

Let's begin with a state-by-state analysis of the way electors have generally voted in the past and what the current polls are showing. Based on that analysis, I will make some predictions. I will categorize each state as **probably going Republican, probably going Democrat,** or as a **"swing state,"** a state that could swing either way.

Alabama - 9 Electoral Votes

The Republican candidate has won every presidential election in Alabama since 1976 when Democrat Jimmy Carter, a Southerner, squeaked out a win in the state.

Romney is leading in all the polls in Alabama.

Romney will win Alabama.

Alaska - 3 Electoral Votes

Alaska has voted for the Republican candidate in every presidential election since 1964 when Democrat Lyndon Johnson won.

Romney will win Alaska.

Arizona - 11 Electoral Votes

Except for 1996, when Democrat Bill Clinton, a Southerner, beat Bob Dole, Arizona has voted for the Republican candidate in every presidential election since 1948 when Truman beat Dewey.

Romney is leading in all the polls in Arizona.

Romney will win Arizona.

Arkansas - 6 Electoral Votes

Arkansas voted for the Democrat Jimmy Carter, a Southerner, in 1976. Since then they have been voting for the Republican presidential candidate, except in 1992 and 1996 when they voted for favorite son, Democrat Bill Clinton.

Romney is leading in all the polls in Arkansas.

Romney will win Arkansas.

California - 55 Electoral Votes

California has voted for the Democratic candidate in the last five presidential elections.

Obama is leading in all the polls in California.

Obama will win California.

Colorado - 9 Electoral Votes

Colorado has a long history of voting for the Republican candidate in presidential elections. However, Clinton won in 1992 (but not in 1996), and in 2008 the state went to Obama.

Currently, Obama is leading Romney in the polls, but Romney is closing the gap.

In 2012, Colorado will be one of the swing states that will decide the election.

Connecticut - 7 Electoral Votes

Connecticut voted for the Democratic candidate in the last five presidential elections.

Obama is leading in all the polls in Connecticut.

Obama will win Connecticut.

Delaware - 3 Electoral Votes

Delaware has been voting for the Democratic candidate in the last five presidential elections.

Obama will win Delaware.

Florida - 29 Electoral Votes

Now we come to the state that caused so much controversy and consternation during the 2000 presidential election. Florida has a long history of voting for the conservative presidential candidate. However, in 1996, they voted for Southerner Bill Clinton, and in 2000, as we have seen, the Democratic candidate got *at least* half the votes in the state.

So far, Obama is leading in the polls, but it is close and Romney is closing the gap.

As in 2000, how Florida votes this time may again determine who the next president will be.

Georgia - 16 Electoral Votes

Except for 1992, when Democratic Bill Clinton, a Southerner, squeaked out a close win, Georgia has voted for the Republican candidate in the last seven presidential elections.

Romney is leading in all the polls in Georgia.

Romney will win Georgia.

Hawaii - 4 Electoral Votes

The island state of Hawaii has voted for the Democratic candidate in the past six presidential elections.

Obama is leading in all the polls in Hawaii.

Obama will win his birth state of Hawaii.

Idaho - 4 Electoral Votes

Idaho has voted for the Republican candidate in the last ten presidential elections.

Romney will win Idaho.

Illinois - 21 Electoral Votes

Illinois is a populous state with a lot of electoral votes. For the past five elections, the state has gone to the Democratic candidate; however, in the five presidential elections before 1992, the state went to the Republican candidate. When Democrat Carter won the presidency in 1976, the state went for Republican Gerald Ford. So it's a bit hard to say which way the state will go in 2012.

The trick to figuring out who will win Illinois in 2012 is to analyze the state's voting history county by county. As of the last census, Cook County (Chicago and environs) had a population of 5,200,950. The entire rest of the state has only 7,668,307 people. Chicago almost always votes for the Democratic candidate; therefore, the question is, can the Republican candidate get enough votes in the rest of the state to overcome that Cook Country Democratic lead? In the last close presidential election in 2000, over 20 downstate counties -- in addition to Cook county -- went for the Democratic candidate Al Gore, thus assuring Gore a close victory in Illinois. Can Obama also win those 20+ downstate counties in 2012? That will determine which way Illinois goes.

Right now, the polls in Illinois are mixed. Some say Romney has the lead, others say Obama has the lead. All the polls agree that it is going to be close.

However, Chicago's powerful Democratic political machine should be able to deliver Chicago and enough downstate votes to pull out a close one. And Illinois is Obama's home state.

Obama will win Illinois.

Indiana - 11 Electoral Votes

Indian is another state that is going to be hard to figure out which way they will vote in 2012. In 2008, Obama squeaked out a very close win (Obama won by 28,391 votes out of a total vote of 2,756,340). But in the nine presidential elections before that, the state always went for the Republican presidential candidate.

Romney is leading in all the polls in Indiana.

In 2012, Indiana will be one of the swing states that will decide the election.

Iowa - 6 Electoral Votes

Iowa is another state that is hard to call. In 1948, the state went for the Democrat Truman, in a close election that mirrored the indecision seen throughout the country that year. After that, they generally voted Republican. But then Democrat Johnson won in 1964. After that, Iowa went back to voting for the Republican presidential candidate until 1988, when they started voting for the Democratic presidential candidate. In 2000, they voted against Bush, but for him in 2004. In 2008, they reversed course again and went for Obama. So which way will they go in 2012? Hard to say, but one thing we can be sure of, it will be close.

As for the polls, most show Obama ahead with Romney closing. However, the Des Moines Register, one of Iowa's most read newspapers, has Romney already in the lead.

In 2012, Iowa will be one of the swing states that will decide the election.

Kansas - 6 Electoral Votes

Kansas has voted for the Republican candidate in the last eleven presidential elections, and 2012 will be no different.

Romney is leading in all the polls in Kansas.

Romney will win Kansas.

Kentucky - 8 Electoral Votes

Kentucky has voted for the Republican candidate in every presidential election except when they voted for Democrat Southerners Clinton and Carter.

Romney is leading in all the polls in Kentucky.

Romney will win Kentucky.

Louisiana - 8 Electoral Votes

Louisiana has voted for the Republican candidate in every presidential election except when they voted for Democrat Southerners Clinton and Carter.

Romney is leading in all the polls in Louisiana.

Romney will win Louisiana.

Maine- 4 Electoral Votes

Maine has voted for the Democratic candidate in the last five presidential elections and there is no reason to think the 2012 election will be any different.

Obama is leading in all the polls in Maine. However, Maine is one of only two states (with Nebraska) that does not use the winner-take-all method of assigning electoral votes. Obama will win Maine, but Romney might pick up one electoral vote there.

Maryland - 10 Electoral Votes

Maryland has voted for the Democratic candidate in the past five presidential elections.

Obama is leading in all the polls in Maryland.

Obama will win Maryland.

Massachusetts - 11 Electoral Votes

Massachusetts has voted for the Democratic candidate in the past six presidential elections. Although Romney, the former governor of the state, still has some support there, it seems likely that the state will continue to vote for the Democratic candidate.

Obama is leading in all the polls in Massachusetts.

Obama will win Massachusetts.

Michigan - 16 Electoral Votes

Michigan voted for the Democratic candidate in the past five presidential elections. However, the economy in Michigan is still suffering, and Romney has some strength there. Much of the vote *for* Obama in 2008 might have been more of a vote *against* Bush.

Romney is leading in all the polls in Michigan.

Michigan will be closer than many people think, and it may end up being one of the swing states that will decide the election.

Minnesota - 10 Electoral Votes

Although Minnesota has voted for the Democratic candidate in the last nine presidential elections, Obama's lead was not all that great in the last election.

Obama is leading in the polls, but not by all that much.

Obama will probably hold onto Minnesota, but by not as great a margin as many expect.

Mississippi - 6 Electoral Votes

Mississippi has voted for the Republican candidate in each of the last eight presidential elections.

Romney is leading in all the polls in Mississippi.

Romney will win Mississippi.

Missouri - 10 Electoral Votes

Missouri has voted for the Republican candidate in the last three presidential elections. They voted against Obama in 2008, but so far, the polls in Missouri are mixed.

In 2012, Missouri will be one of the swing states that will decide the election.

Montana - 3 Electoral Votes

Montana has voted for the Republican candidate in nine out of the past ten presidential elections (Clinton beat Bush in 1992).

Romney is leading in all the polls in Montana.

Romney will win Montana.

Nebraska - 5 Electoral Votes

Nebraska has voted for the Republican candidate in the last eleven presidential elections.

However, Nebraska is one of only two states (with Maine) that does not use the winner-take-all method of assigning electoral votes. In the 2008 election, McCain won the state, but Obama received enough votes to pick up one electoral vote (undoubtedly due to anti-Bush voters).

Romney is leading in all the polls in Nebraska.

Romney will win Nebraska.

Nevada - 6 Electoral Votes

Nevada has a mixed pattern of voting. They voted for Obama in 2008, but they voted for Bush in the two prior elections. They voted for Democratic Clinton in 1992 and 1996, but they voted for the Republican candidate in the five presidential elections before that.

Obama is leading in all the polls in Nevada, but it is close and Romney is gaining.

At this time, Nevada is too close to call.

In 2012, it may be one of the swing states that will decide the election.

New Hampshire - 4 Electoral Votes

New Hampshire has a history of being a swing state. However, it went for Obama in 2008, and so far, Obama is leading in all the polls in New Hampshire.

Obama will win New Hampshire.

New Jersey - 14 Electoral Votes

New Jersey has voted for the Democratic candidate in the last five presidential elections.

Romney is leading in all the polls in the six prior elections.

Nevertheless, Obama is leading in all the polls there.

Obama will likely win New Jersey.

New Mexico - 5 Electoral Votes

New Mexico went for Obama in 2009, but the state went for Bush in 2004 in an extremely close race (Bush won by only 5,988 votes). In 2000, Gore won the state by only 366 votes (out of 598,605 votes cast).

Obama is leading in the polls, but Romney is gaining.

46% of New Mexico's citizens are of Hispanic descent. If either candidate wants to win New Mexico, they will have to win the Hispanic vote.

In 2012, New Mexico will be one of the swing states that will decide the election.

New York - 29 Electoral Votes

New York has voted for the Democratic candidate in the last six presidential elections.

Obama is leading in all the polls there.

Obama will win New York.

North Carolina - 15 Electoral Votes

In 2008, Obama beat McCain in North Carolina, but only by 14,177 votes (out of 4,310,789 votes cast). However, North Carolina voted for the Republican candidate in the seven presidential elections before that.

The polls show Romney leading in every poll.

In 2012, North Carolina will revert back to its normal voting pattern and go for the Republican Romney.

North Dakota - 3 Electoral Votes

North Dakota has voted for the Republican candidate in the last eleven presidential elections.

Romney is leading in all the polls in North Dakota.

Romney will win North Dakota.

Ohio - 18 Electoral Votes

Ohio voted for Obama in 2008, but it was close. The state went for Bush in the two prior elections, but went for Democratic Clinton in the two elections before that.

So far, Obama is leading in the polls in Ohio, but Romney is closing.

In 2012, Ohio could be one of the swing states that will decide the election.

Oklahoma - 7 Electoral Votes

Oklahoma has voted for the Republican candidate in the last eleven presidential elections.

Romney will win Oklahoma.

Oregon - 7 Electoral Votes

Oregon has voted for the Democratic candidate in the past six presidential elections.

Obama is leading in all the polls in Oregon.

Obama will win Oregon.

Pennsylvania - 20 Electoral Votes

Pennsylvania has voted for the Democratic candidate in the last five presidential elections.

Obama is leading in all the polls in Pennsylvania.

Obama will win Pennsylvania.

Rhode Island - 4 Electoral Votes

Rhode Island has voted for the Democratic candidate in the last six presidential elections

Obama will win Rhode Island.

South Carolina - 9 Electoral Votes

South Carolina has voted for the Republican candidate in the last eight presidential elections.

Romney is leading in all the polls in South Carolina.

Romney will win South Carolina.

South Dakota - 3 Electoral Votes

South Dakota has voted for the Republican candidate in the last eleven presidential elections.

Romney will win South Dakota.

Tennessee - 11 Electoral Votes

Except for 1992 and 1996, when the state went for Democrat Southerner Bill Clinton, Tennessee has voted for the Republican candidate in every presidential election since Southerner Jimmy Carter won in 1976.

Romney will win Tennessee.

Texas - 38 Electoral Votes

Texas has voted for the Republican candidate in the last eight presidential elections.

Romney is leading in all the polls in Texas.

Romney will win Texas.

Utah - 6 Electoral Votes

Utah has voted for the Republican candidate in the last eleven presidential elections.

Mormon Romney will win Utah, the Mormon state.

Vermont - 3 Electoral Votes

Vermont has voted for the Democratic candidate in the past five presidential elections.

Obama is leading in all the polls in Vermont.

Obama will win Vermont.

Virginia - 13 Electoral Votes

In 2008, Obama won the Virginia presidential election by a very close vote. However, Virginia voted for the Republican candidate in the prior ten presidential elections.

Romney is leading in the polls in Virginia, but it is close.

In 2012, Virginia could be one of the swing states that will decide the election.

Washington - 12 Electoral Votes

Washington has voted for the Democratic candidate in the past six presidential elections.

Obama is leading in all the polls in Washington.

Obama will win Washington.

Washington D. C. - 3 Electoral Votes

It required an amendment to the United States Constitution (the Twenty-Third Amendment) in 1961 to give the citizens of the District of Columbia any say in who got to be president and vice president (they are still not allowed to vote for representatives or senators). The amendment restricts Washington D.C. to three electoral votes, no matter how many people live there.

The first presidential election in which they got to vote president and vice president was in 1964. They voted for the Democratic candidate, Lyndon Johnson, and have voted for the Democratic candidate in every presidential election since.

Obama will win Washington D.C.

West Virginia - 5 Electoral Votes

West Virginia has voted for the Republican presidential candidate in the last three elections. In 1992 and 1996, the state went for Democrat Southerner Bill Clinton. In 1998, the state went for

Republican Bush over Democrat Dukakis in a very close vote (Bush won by only 30,951 votes). Nevertheless, the state gave McCain a strong majority over Obama in the last election. There is no reason to believe they would go the other way in the upcoming 2012 election.

Romney will win West Virginia.

Wisconsin -10 Electoral Votes

Wisconsin has voted for the Democratic candidate in the past six presidential elections, but before that they often voted for the Republican candidate.

The Wisconsin polls show Obama ahead, but Romney is closing.

In 2012, Wisconsin could be one of the swing states that will decide the election.

Wyoming - 3 Electoral Votes

Wyoming has voted for the Republican candidate in the last eleven presidential elections.

Romney will win Wyoming.

What It All Adds up To

If we look only at the states where the outcome seems assured, we find 22 states very likely to be in the Romney camp, and 18 states very likely to be in the Obama camp.

But all that tells us is that there are more states that have a long history of voting for the Republican candidate than there are states with a long history of voting for the Democratic candidate. What counts is the Electoral College vote. In the 2008 election McCain won 28 states to Obama's 22 and still lost the election by a considerable margin.

More of the states that are likely to vote for Obama are states with large cities. Large cities mean larger state populations, which means those states have more electoral votes. If we add up the electoral votes in the 22 states we've put in the **Romney camp**, we get **185 electoral votes**. If we add up the electoral votes in the 18 states we've put in the **Obama camp**, we get **220 electoral votes**. As you can see, winning more states doesn't necessarily mean you get more electoral votes.

However, a 220 to 185 vote lead for Obama means little because it takes 270 electoral votes to be elected president, and the eleven still-undecided "swing states" hold 133 electoral votes.

Let's look at each of the swing states to try to get a better idea of which candidate they will go for in November.

Analysis of the Swing States

Colorado

As discussed above, Colorado has a long history of voting for the Republican presidential candidate. However, the state went for Obama in 2008 and the polls are showing Obama ahead right now.

I believe Obama will win Colorado in a close election.

That would bring **Obama's total up to 229 electoral votes**.

Florida

Florida was the final battleground for Electoral College votes in the 2000 election and it may be the battleground for the 2012 election as well. The polls are close and there are enough undecided voters to change the outcome. However, except for 1996 when Florida went for Democrat Southerner Clinton, and the last election when Democrat Obama squeaked out a narrow win, Florida has almost always voted for the Republican presidential candidate.

In 2012, as it was in 2000, the Florida governor is a Republican. That once again may turn out to be one of the most important factors in determining which candidate will win. Rick Scott, a wealthy venture capitalist (like Romney), was recently elected governor running on a very conservative platform. He spent 75 million of his own money to get elected, and he has the support of Jeb Bush, George Bush's brother who was Florida's governor during the controversial Florida 2000 presidential election. In addition, Scott partnered with George W. Bush to buy the Texas Rangers baseball team so he is *in* with the Republican power brokers.

Governor Scott only took office only last year, so it will be an important goal for him to deliver the state for Romney.

Given George Bush and the Republican's historically low approval rating before the last election, I'm going to assume the narrow Florida win for Obama in 2008 was more of an anti-Bush, anti-Republican vote than a true vote for Obama . For all of the reasons above, I predict that Romney will win a narrow victory in Florida and take the state's 29 electoral votes.

That would bring **Romney's total up to 214 electoral votes.**

Indiana

In Indiana, we have three factors to consider: 1) The polls are showing Romney with a slight lead. 2) In 2008, Obama only won Indiana by a minuscule 28,391 votes (out of 2,756,340 votes cast). 3) Obama's 2008 win was the only Democratic win since 1964.

Based on those three factors it seems likely that Obama's 2008 narrow win in Indiana was actually an anti-Bush vote because of the two dragging-on wars and the collapsing economy. One of the wars continues today, and the economy has not improved enough under Obama to make the voters of Indiana happy. Therefore, it seem likely that Indiana will revert back to its Republican tradition and go for Romney.

That would bring **Romney's total up to 225 electoral votes.**

Iowa

Iowa is a tough one to predict. Unlike the other Midwestern states with an agricultural base, Iowa has not always voted for the Republican presidential candidate. Obama won the state in 2008 and he has a slight lead in the polls now. If the citizens of Iowa feel that the economy is improving enough to make them feel better about their lives, they may well go for Obama again in 2012.

That would bring **Obama's total up to 235 electoral votes.**

Michigan

Michigan has been going for the Democratic presidential candidate for the past five elections. However, before 1992, they usually went for the Republican candidate. The crucial factor in the 2012 election will be their weak economy and the resulting very weak housing market in the state.

On the other hand, some of the Michigan auto industry did get bailed out during Obama's term in office.

However, many of the auto industry jobs have been moved out of the country so it is possible some of the bailout money went elsewhere.

Obama has a slight lead in the polls, so the fact that Mitt Romney's father was a former governor of the state may not help Mitt all that much in this election. It will probably be a close win for Obama.

That would bring **Obama's total up to 251 electoral votes.**

Missouri

The polls in Missouri are showing a mixed picture for 2012. The state has voted for the Democratic presidential candidate in the past, but that can be explained by the fact that the candidates were from nearby Southern states (Clinton from Arkansas and Carter from Georgia). The state went for McCain over Obama in 2008, and I believe they will go for Romney over Obama in 2012.

That would bring **Romney's total up to 235 electoral votes.**

Nevada

In a close vote, Obama won Nevada in 2008. However, in the two previous elections, the state went for Bush. The state went for Clinton in 1992 and 1996, but before that the state almost always went for the Republican presidential candidate.

To get a better idea of which way the citizens of Nevada are leaning now, we only have to look at the recent election for governor. Brian Sandoval, a Republican, was elected over Democrat Rory Reid, the Clark County Commissioner and son of U.S. Senate Majority Leader Harry Reid. Sandoval won every county in the state except for Reid's home county, Clark Country. Sandoval just took office last year, and it will be important for him to deliver the state for the Republicans. I believe Romney will squeak out a win in Nevada.

That would bring **Romney's total up to 241 electoral votes.**

New Mexico

New Mexico defines the concept of swing state. They voted for Obama in 2008, but they voted against Bush in 2000. They voted for

Bill Clinton in 1992 and 1996, but before that they almost always voted for the Republican presidential candidate.

Romney is leading in the polls, but Romney is closing.

This state seemed like a toss-up, until the most recent election for governor. Susana Martinez, a Hispanic and a Republican, became the state's first female governor. She just took office last year and is now already being talked about as a potential running mate for Mitt Romney in 2012. Even if she is not chosen as Romney's running mate for 2012, it will be very important for her to deliver the state for the Republicans.

Therefore, I will predict a **very** close win for Romney in New Mexico.

That would bring **Romney's total up to 246 electoral votes.**

Ohio

Obama won Ohio in 2008, but only by 262,224 votes (out of 5,721,815 votes cast). Ohio usually votes for the Republican presidential candidate, but they did vote twice for Bill Clinton.

The manufacturing segment of Ohio's economy is still suffering (which might well be why they voted against Bush in 2008).

The mood of the voters of Ohio can best be judged by looking at the recent election for governor. John Kasich, a Republican, defeated the Democratic incumbent.

Kasich just took office last year, and it will be important for him to deliver the state for the Republicans in 2012.

I believe Ohio will revert back to its tradition of voting for Republican candidates.

Romney will win Ohio in a close election.

That would bring **Romney's total up to 264 electoral votes, very close to the 270 needed to win the presidency.**

Virginia

Although Obama won the close 2008 vote in Virginia, the state has gone for the Republican candidate in every election before that all the way back to 1964.

The polls are mixed, but I believe Virginia will revert to its traditional voting pattern and go for Romney in 2012.

That would bring **Romney's total up to 277 electoral votes, six more than is needed to win the presidency.**

Wisconsin

Wisconsin has a history of voting for the Democratic presidential candidate. However, they recently elected a very conservative Republican governor, Scott Walker, who just took office last year.

In Wisconsin, the election of 2012 will take place in a climate of controversy as Governor Walker will be fighting for his office against a recall effort that has drawn national attention. That may pull some attention away from the weak economy in the state, and it will motivate the Democratic voters to get out and vote.

Despite the fact that the state recently elected a conservative Republican governor, I believe Wisconsin will vote for the Democratic presidential candidate as it has for the past six elections.

That would bring **Obama's total up to 261 electoral votes.**

The Results of the 2012 Presidential Election

Based on my analysis, Romney will gather enough electoral votes to win the election.

However, my analysis also reveals that Obama will win the states with the largest populations, and even in the states he loses, he will gain a large number of votes. Therefore, it seem likely that **Obama will win the popular vote, but because of the biased weighting of the Electoral College, Romney will be the forty fifth president of the United States.** Obama may win the popular vote by a million votes or more, but lose in the Electoral College by only a few votes

But as we have learned, the popular vote is irrelevant. **It is only the vote of the Electoral College that counts.**

If Obama really does lose the presidency despite wining the popular vote by that large a margin, at least we can hope that it will finally galvanize the effort to get rid of the Electoral College once and for all.

To completely get rid of the Electoral College would take a Constitutional amendment. That is unlikely to happen because such an amendment would have to be ratified by three-fourths of the states;

at least some of the states with smaller populations would have to give up their advantage in the selection of presidents.

However, there is another solution: the states could stop using the winner-take-all system and instead assign electoral votes proportionally as Maine and Nebraska do. There have been a number of proposals in many states to do just that.

But would the Republicans be willing to change to proportionally-assigned Electoral College voting for the good of the country? We shall see.

What Could Change the 2012 Election Outcome?

Of course, a significant national or world event could change things, depending on how President Obama reacted to it.

Another thing that might complicate the election would be the emergence of **a strong third-party candidate**. However, for Romney to lose, **it would have to be a popular conservative candidate** who could pull votes away from Romney, and so far such a candidate has not come forward.

If a third-party candidate could somehow take eight electoral votes away from Romney, **it would send the election to the House of Representatives**. Right now, the Republicans control the House, 242 to 193. If we use the election of 1924 as a guide, there is no reason to believe the House Republicans would vote for Obama just because he won the popular vote.

However, it is important to remember that in such a circumstance, each **state** gets one vote, no matter how large or small the state's population. That means at least 26 states would have to agree on one candidate. By my analysis of the makeup of the current House of Representatives, Romney would win 29 states, and Obama would win 21, and Romney would be determined the winner.

So in either circumstance, an Electoral College decision, or a House of Representatives decision, by my analysis, the winner of the popular vote, Obama, will not get to be president.

Chapter Seventeen
What We Have Learned

As we have learned, the delegates to the **constitutional convention** in 1787 didn't think the citizens of the United States should be allowed to vote for the office of president. After extended discussion and controversy, **the Electoral College system** of electing the president was approved as a compromise. Two hundred years later, it is still the system we use today.

The basic concept of the Electoral College system is that the states decide who they want to be president, then they **send electors** to the nation's capital to inform the government of their decision. In other words, **the framers of the Constitution left it up to the political leaders of the states to decide who the president would be**. The candidate who came in second got to be the vice president.

But the people of the United States didn't like not being able to vote for their president. They demanded a popular vote. **One by one, the states, began to hold a popular vote for president, even though it didn't really count.** The political leaders of the states still determined who the electors would be, and even then, the electors that were sent to the capital were not required to vote for the candidate they were pledged to.

Eventually, under pressure from the electorate, the political leaders in the states began to use the results of the popular vote as at least a guide to who they should elect as president.

The crafters of the Constitution didn't anticipate the emergence of political parties. So when, in the presidential election of 1800, the new political parties cast votes for their two preferred candidates, as required by the Constitution. **That sent the decision to the House of Representatives.**

The political leaders demanded a change to the Electoral College system. The leaders of the political parties wanted to vote for the president and vice president separately.

In 1803, an amendment to the Constitution to change the Electoral College system was passed to correct that oversight about how electors voted for president and vice president. However, no other aspect of the Electoral College system was changed. **The political leaders still didn't want the people voting for president directly.**

At the Constitution Convention in 1787, another contentious issue was how many representatives each state got to send to the House of Representatives through local elections. Because each state got to send representatives based on the state's population, there was contention over whether the Southern states got to count their slaves as part of their population (even though they didn't have legal status as citizens). In a compromise with the South, the Northern states agreed to **allow the Southern states to count each of their millions of slaves as three-fifth of a person**. That gave the Southern slave states considerably more power in the House of Representatives.

A senate was created as a governing body with power equal to the House of Representatives, but in another compromise with the small states, each state got to send two senators to the senate no matter what the population of the state was. However, unlike the House of Representatives, the **senators would not be elected but would be appointed by the political leaders in the states**.

One of the last decisions to be made was **how to elect the president**. It was the most contentious of all the debates. Most of the delegates to the Constitution Convention assumed the president would be elected just as representatives to the House were. But many of the delegates from the smaller-population states disagreed. They felt general elections would give the larger states more power in determining who the president would be.

In the end, **another compromise was worked out creating the Electoral College system**. Each state, no matter how large or how small, would get to send a number of electors based on the number of members that state had in Congress. That meant, even states with very small populations got to send at least three electors. Today, there are seven states that get to send three electors, even though those states have relatively few residents.

The problems of **unfairness in the Electoral College system** were compounded when some **states adopted a winner-takes-all system** of assigning electoral votes. In defense, most of the other states also had to also switch to the winner-takes-all system (Today, only Maine and Nebraska use the proportional system of allocating electoral votes).

The winner-takes-all system is extremely unfair because the people who voted for the less popular candidate **get no credit for their vote at all**. All votes for the losing candidate get thrown out. In fact, if you know the candidate you favor is sure to win your state, what is the point of voting at all?

Over the years, **the Electoral College system of electing a president has failed to agree with the popular vote for president four times:**

- In 1824, **Andrew Jackson** won the popular vote convincingly, but **John Quincy Adams** made deals in Congress to be selected president.

- In 1876, in the tumultuous years after the Civil War, **Samuel J. Tilden** won both the popular vote and the Electoral College vote, but claims of voter fraud in the South negated his win and **Rutherford B. Hayes** was named president.

- In 1888, **Grover Cleveland** ran for reelection and won the popular vote. However, Republican **Benjamin Harrison** eked out a narrow Electoral College win and was made president.

- In 2000, **George Bush** became president even though **Al Gore** won the general election by 543,895 votes.

The only reason that kind of situation hasn't happened more often is because the presidential elections have not been close. Now that the two main parties are closer in popularity, the advantage of the smaller-population states is starting to show up more often. In every close election from now on, it will undoubtedly be **the smaller states that will determine the winner**, meaning it will be **more likely that the winner of the popular vote will not get to be president.**

Conclusions

The main conclusion is clear: **the Electoral College system of electing presidents often fails to elect the people's choice**. The Electoral College system was **designed from the beginning to take the decision about who the president will be out of the hands of the people**.

With the Electoral College system in place as it is today, the winner of the popular vote may not get to be president, even if he or she wins by a very large majority. Why? Because a vote in a state with a small population counts for more in the Electoral College than a vote in a state with a large population. If we continue to have close elections, **the smaller states will continue to determine who the president will be** no matter how many votes a presidential candidate wins in the popular election.

If what happened in 2000 happens again in 2012, **will the people rise up** and demand a change? They didn't in 2000 when the presidential candidate who won the general election by more than half a million votes was not allowed to take his rightful place as the president of the United States. If it happens again this time, will anybody care? Will the people demand the right to directly elect our presidents? We shall see.

INDEX

About The Author

Dr. Everett Murdock is an Emeritus Professor at California State University, Long Beach.